LIVING *and* LEADING *from Your*

HOLY Discontent

Books by Bill Hybels

Holy Discontent

Just Walk Across the Room

The Volunteer Revolution

Courageous Leadership

Rediscovering Church (with Lynne Hybels)

Honest to God?

Fit to Be Tied (with Lynne Hybels)

Descending Into Greatness (with Rob Wilkins)

Becoming a Contagious Christian (with Mark Mittelberg and Lee Strobel)

The New Community Series (with Kevin and Sherry Harney)

Colossians

James

1 Peter

Philippians

Romans

Sermon on the Mount 1

Sermon on the Mount 2

The InterActions Small Group Series (with Kevin and Sherry Harney)

Authenticity	*Love in Action*
Character	*Marriage*
Commitment	*Meeting God*
Community	*New Identity*
Essential Christianity	*Parenting*
Fruit of the Spirit	*Prayer*
Getting a Grip	*Reaching Out*
Jesus	*The Real Deal*
Lessons on Love	*Significance*
Living in God's Power	*Transformation*

LIVING *and* LEADING *from Your*

HOLY
Discontent

A Companion Guide for Ministry Leaders

BILL HYBELS
with
Ashley Wiersma

Living and Leading from Your Holy Discontent
Copyright © 2007 by Bill Hybels

Requests for information should be addressed to:
Zondervan, Grand Rapids, Michigan 49530

ISBN-10: 0-310-28290-X
ISBN-13: 978-0-310-28290-7

Interior design by 32 design

Printed in the United States of America

07 08 09 10 11 12 13 · 10 9 8 7 6 5 4 3 2 1

Contents

GETTING STARTED

Welcome to *Living and Leading from Holy Discontent: A Companion Guide for Ministry Leaders*. Over the course of the coming days and weeks, you will discover how to approach your leadership role with unprecedented energy, enthusiasm, and passion for the cause that compelled you into ministry to begin with—pointing lost people to faith in God, growing up believers into mature followers of Christ, and resourcing the needs of marginalized people.

Intended Use

Before working through this companion guide, it is best to read the book on which it is based: *Holy Discontent: Fueling the Firestorm That Ignites Personal Vision*. The book presents the helpful framework of "finding and feeding" holy discontent, while this guide offers practical guidance to show you the exact steps to take.

This guide is designed to be an individual processing tool. If you want to work through this material with your core team, each person should have his or her own copy of *Living and Leading from Your Holy Discontent*. And I encourage you to work through the book with your team. If everyone is focused on working through the same subject matter at once, you will achieve greater impact in leveraging holy discontent across your ministry.

Format

Presented in three parts, this guide reveals that in order to *live and lead from* holy discontent, ministry leaders must:

- **Illuminate** their own holy discontent and learn how to communicate it to those they lead (Part I).

- **Invigorate** holy discontent in others, including those they lead and those to whom they report (Part II).

- **Instigate** connecting the dots of holy discontent among their team (Part III).

Living and Leading from Your Holy Discontent includes interactive processing exercises that encourage you to ask the tough questions of your ministry strategy, your supporting organizational structure, and the key people with whom you collaborate. In addition, insightful prompts help you act on what you learn, and space is provided for personal reflection.

Work at your own pace. Do parts of a chapter once a day, work through a whole chapter in a week, or give yourself more time to mull over each chapter. It may be helpful to set aside a specific time to work through the material, for example, during your quiet time each morning, on your day off each week, or on a predetermined set of days throughout the month. Whatever your pace, give the material your full attention when you do choose to engage it.

May you be blessed as you find freedom to pursue your unique, God-given passions, and may you be strengthened as you discover the necessary tools for converting *frustration* about what's at odds in this world into *fuel* you need to make a radical difference in your own life, as well as in the lives of those you lead and serve.

Part I

ILLUMINATE
Your Holy Discontent

FIND IT

After more than three decades spent observing leaders, learning from leaders, working alongside leaders, and training leaders, I've come to the conclusion that the most effective, energetic, motivated, purpose-filled leaders I know are the ones who live and lead from the energy of their holy discontent. Likewise, the most ineffective, deflated, unmotivated, disheartened leaders I know are those who don't.

Allow me to explain.

I believe there is something *every* leader was born to do, and that the leadership role they fill is the God-given vehicle through which they will do it. When leaders take pains to figure out their "one thing" and then feed it consistently so that it keeps growing and growing in their lives, they actually tap into an *alternative fuel source* that never has to dry up. What ministry leader doesn't need that type of supernatural reserve?

What's more, I believe ministry leaders owe it to themselves, those they lead, and God himself to tap into their "holy discontent" fuel. Simply put, the stakes are too high for leaders to give the cause of Christ anything less than their most energized, purpose-filled best!

Through a series of thought-provoking questions and interactive exercises, this companion guide is intended to help you do just that. Regardless how full your ministry fuel tank feels today, it will absolutely top out when you commit yourself afresh to finding—and then feeding—your holy discontent. This is the subject of Part I, "Illuminate Your Holy Discontent."

Ready to dive in?

THE RIPPLE EFFECT

A decade or so ago, I began to devote more intentional time to training senior pastors and other ministry leaders in smaller group settings. The shift in priorities was born out of my deep-seated belief that if you can change the heart of a leader, then you can change an entire church. If you can change a church, then the neighborhood gets changed. Change a neighborhood, and you can change a city. Change a city, and you can change a nation. Change a nation, and you can change the entire world!

To put this powerful progression into your own context, note the areas that stand to be influenced by your effective, God-honoring leadership:

LEADERSHIP'S RIPPLE EFFECT

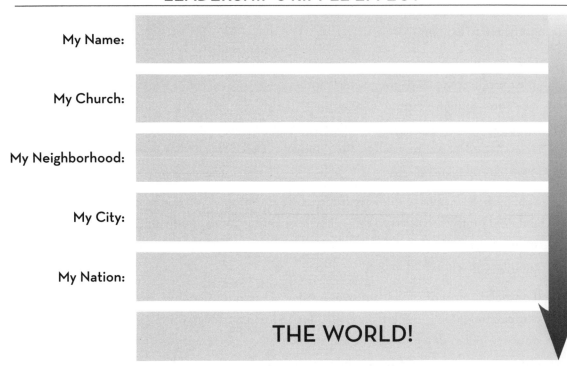

My Name:

My Church:

My Neighborhood:

My City:

My Nation:

THE WORLD!

When leaders lead well, this ripple effect flows beautifully. In fact, when leaders stay connected to their holy discontent, they can then approach ministry with boundless energy and enthusiasm to see the whole world impacted by the Good News of the Gospel. They operate from a context of *abundance*, which is precisely what Christ intended.

Jesus Christ promised that for everyone who would follow him, an abundant life awaited, a reality in which things like grace and peace and rest could abound (John 10:10). I have been involved in ministry leadership since my early twenties, and when I look back on my journey, I see evidence of these "episodes of abundance" having surfaced all along the way.

> *When leaders stay connected to their holy discontent, they can then approach ministry with boundless energy and enthusiasm to see the whole world impacted by the Good News of the Gospel. They operate from a context of abundance, which is precisely what Christ intended.*

REMEMBER EPISODES OF ABUNDANCE

The time when I most powerfully experienced God's grace, for example, occurred right after I was converted. I had been subscribing to the self-help plan until that point, but in what I have frequently described as some strange "amazing grace attack," I turned things over to God. I realized I couldn't earn my way into his favor—or his kingdom—and so I accepted his gift of grace and charted a new course for my life, one that allowed *him* to sit in the driver's seat.

Whether you have been leading for thirty days or thirty years, perhaps you too have known episodes of abundance at various points along the path of your leadership journey. As you seek out your holy discontent, remember what those experiences felt like!

Note your experience with each episode listed on the chart on the following page, as well as when you experienced it and the circumstances surrounding the occasion. I included my "grace" example to get you started.

I bring up these episodes of abundance because, especially for leaders, it's all too easy to succumb to scarcity thinking in ministry. It's a disturbing trend that seems to be on the rise: while most ministry leaders believe living an "abundant" kind of life is *possible* (Christ says so, right?), given the stresses and demands of ministry, for many of us, it just doesn't seem very *probable*.

MY EPISODES OF ABUNDANCE

	Promise of Abundant Living I Experienced	When I Experienced It	Circumstances Surrounding It
Ex.	Grace	On a hillside in Wisconsin at age 17	I had just surrendered my life to Christ
	Grace		
	Peace		
	Rest		
	Purpose		

LEARN FROM SEASONS OF STRUGGLE

As I interact with senior leaders these days, here are the seasons of struggle I'm hearing with greater and greater frequency:

"I've hit my leadership limit. I can't cope with the pressure, and I have nobody left to talk to. Please help me."

"To be painfully candid, I think I've taken this church as far as I can take it. I wonder if my job here is done."

"My calling has been uprooted. I feel like I'm spinning my wheels here, and I can't imagine this is what God had in mind for me when he called me into full-time ministry."

"I'm exhausted, but I can't rest. I'm dying inside but can't get off the treadmill long enough to do anything about it."

"In all honesty, I've done everything I know to do, but this congregation is just not buying the vision I know God is selling me on."

"If my senior staff only knew the balls I am already juggling on behalf of this church . . . they have no clue how utterly overwhelmed I feel."

"I've lost heart. I can't remember the last time I had it, but it's long gone now."

One Pastor's Journey

One of these comments is from a senior pastor I met a few years ago. At the time, the visible signs of his ministry "success" were strong: attendance was up; giving figures were up; he had recently made two fantastic hires to fill pivotal senior leadership roles; he was preparing to launch a satellite campus across town; and he seemed well poised to enter a scheduled capital campaign the following year that would pay down old debt and cover expansion at the current facility.

Everything looked rosy, but internally, he admitted, he was suffering a slow and agonizing leadership death. Twenty-plus years of ministry had taken a toll, and his fuel reserves felt all dried up. He cast vision but noticed that even his senior staff seemed uninspired by it, which caused him constantly to question his original calling: Was he really supposed to be leading these people at this time? Was he supposed to be leading at all?

Each week he was pulled in two dozen highly important, highly urgent directions and consistently felt like a firefighter instead of a pastor. He spent less time with the weekend service planning team—one of the few groups that tapped into his vast artistic energies—and more time beside hospital beds or officiating funerals, despite his evident lack of gifts for such work. When he finally slumped into bed each night and considered the next day's demands, he was so weary and despondent that he wondered if somewhere along the way he had slid into a serious state of clinical depression. Increasingly, he pulled away emotionally and physically from his leadership team and from other staff and key volunteers, believing that perhaps a little distance would make matters better.

In the years since our first conversation, it appears little to nothing in his reality has shifted. He's still fighting to keep his nose above water, treading for all he is worth but hardly living out the abundance Christ affords.

Your Own Journey

If you're like me, then you probably relate to this pastor's dilemma more than you care to admit! Seasons of struggle are inevitable for every leader; it goes with the territory. Are any of the following statements reflective of the current season you find yourself in?

These days . . .

- ❏ I am more reactive than proactive in my leadership.
- ❏ My passion for the role has flat-lined.
- ❏ I feel blurry about my ministry vision.
- ❏ I feel unsupported in my ministry vision.
- ❏ My energy supply is tapped out.
- ❏ The chasm seems to be widening between my gift mix and my job responsibilities.
- ❏ I've got doubts regarding my original calling.
- ❏ I often feel conflicted about my top priorities.
- ❏ The desire for mental distance from my role and/or physical distance from the people I lead and serve is stronger and stronger.

Whether you checked nine of the boxes or none of them, you probably agree that "weary and despondent" is a difficult way to do life, not to mention ministry! When you feel stuck in those seasons of struggle, everything around you, *including* you, takes the hit. In the space provided on the next page, write down the hits you've experienced during such seasons on the following areas of your life and ministry.

Myself

My family

My ministry vision

The people I lead or serve

ACKNOWLEDGE THE TOUGH STUFF OF MINISTRY

Ministry is tough! In fact, ministry has *always* been tough. It was tough for Jesus, and it was tough for the very first church leaders he rallied around his cause. If you'll recall, they were an untrained, unsophisticated, unexpected assortment of people (including his mom and a dozen cohorts known as "disciples") who were totally unaware of what lay ahead.

Ministry leadership was certainly no cakewalk for those folks. Think about it: Early church leaders worked on behalf of a highly controversial figure who would be crucified because of his radical beliefs; they were asked to sacrifice their families, their occupations, their reputations, and their routines in order to pursue their leadership roles; and to top it off, their contribution in the neighboring areas they visited was often greeted with ridicule, beatings, stoning . . . even death.

In Matthew 10:16, Jesus sends out his twelve disciples as "sheep among wolves," meaning, pretty much, that they should get prepared to take a pounding. I envision the disciples heading to their huts after that little pow-wow with wobbly knees and a refreshed desire to pray for some power! When I feel like a "sheep among wolves," my proneness to bend a knee and ask for God's aid sure skyrockets. For me, the worst part of those seasons of struggle is that I know I'm not living out the promises of transformation a relationship with Christ offers. Instead of tapping into divine promises of provision and peace and well-being, I'm truncating my Christian experience and settling instead for a posture born of this world.

Perhaps you too have experienced this dichotomy; for example, what

> "Early church leaders worked on behalf of a highly controversial figure who would be crucified because of his radical beliefs; they were asked to sacrifice their families, their occupations, their reputations, and their routines in order to pursue their leadership roles; and to top it off, their contribution in the neighboring areas they visited was often greeted with ridicule, beatings, stoning . . . even death."

contrasts would surface if you were to evaluate the promises you noted in the table on page 14 in light of some of the tough stuff of ministry you have faced? For example, despite my grasp of grace at a young age, during a few tough seasons of leadership, I've found myself wanting works-based approval from God or others. Although Christ promises rest, I've known times in ministry of sheer exhaustion. I could go on and on with examples, but how about you take a turn.

Christ promises _____,

but I've experienced _____.

Christ promises _____,

but I've experienced _____.

Christ promises _____,

but I've experienced _____.

Christ promises _____,

but I've experienced _____.

Christ promises _____,

but I've experienced _____.

For leaders, acknowledging a list like this can be difficult or even devastating. Wherever you land, I hope you'll keep reading. The life of abundance Christ promises is not a pipe dream. It's real. It's accessible. And your holy discontent can lead you right to it.

GET FUELED BY HOLY DISCONTENT

Although it is impossible to extract every tough thing from ministry leadership, it is *altogether* possible to experience ministry with a topped-off fuel tank. Frustrations will always abound that threaten to rob your joy, cripple your effectiveness, dilute your focus, and permanently take you out of the game. But as you read in *Holy Discontent*, "Once that frustration and anger is understood as being your *holy discontent*—your spiritual connection to the God who's working to fix everything—it's as if an enormous wave of positive energy gets released inside you. . . . This energy causes you to act on the dissatisfaction that's been brewing deep within your soul and compels you to say yes to joining forces with God so that the darkness and depravity around you gets pushed back."[1]

When you live and lead from the fuel of your holy discontent, the "supernatural supply of energy allows you to move forward past all the natural human-nature responses and enter instead into a life viewed from God's point of view. In other words, your perspective shifts from that which your eyes can see to that which God *tells you is true*. And it is in *this* reality that what is enslaved can still be set free, what is broken can still be mended, what is diseased can still be restored, what is hated can still be loved, what is dirty can still be made clean, and what is wrong can still be made right."[2]

Jesus' Holy Discontent Fuel

Jesus himself was fueled for ministry by his holy discontent, which is recorded in John 18:37. "The reason I was born and came into the world," Jesus said, "is to testify to the truth."

Jesus' holy discontent was sparked by an insatiable desire to declare truth. He was utterly determined to expose every lie, every ounce of deception, and every manipulative tactic. As a result, I imagine he sat up in heaven, just watching the worsening conditions

> *When you live and lead from the fuel of your holy discontent, the "supernatural supply of energy allows you to move forward past all the natural, human-nature responses and enter instead into a life viewed from God's point of view. In other words, your perspective shifts from that which your eyes can see to that which God tells you is true."*

unfold on planet Earth, saying, "I can't *stand* this! I can't *stand* Satan's lies and the horribly damaging effects they're having on my people's minds and hearts!" Finally, when his frustration had reached fever pitch, God gave Jesus the nod, and he was off!

God hated lies and deception. Jesus hated lies and deception. And together, they were going to do something about it.

Jesus came to testify to the truth, he lived a perfect life in defense of the truth, and he died an agonizing death on behalf of the truth.

The First Believers' Holy Discontent Fuel

Then, just seven weeks later, Acts 2:42–47 records the incredible events that unfolded at Pentecost. Think back on that little company of believers who crossed the line of faith that day. Based on what you know of the passage, in what ways did these Christ-followers "do ministry" despite the tough stuff they faced?

When they came across sick people, they . . .

When they learned of a pressing financial need, they . . .

When they locked eyes with people in bondage, they . . .

When they encountered lonely people, they . . .

Those first-century believers had seen Jesus participate in his Father's kingdom-building activity and were utterly compelled to follow suit. They saw that when Jesus was faithful to do his Father's bidding, aspects of abundance surfaced. Suddenly, Jesus possessed strength to deny Satan a foothold; grace and power to fend off persecution; energy to work hard each day; enthusiasm to fire up those around him; passion to pursue the vision with his whole heart; perfect peace to fulfill the role God had asked him to play.

"If we can get our own passions lined up with the passions of God," those first church leaders must have thought, "then we can live out this abundance-life too!"

God hated to see his people afflicted, and so those Acts 2 leaders alleviated human suffering. God despised selfishness, and so they shared their possessions. God disapproved of isolationism, and so they welcomed strangers into their fellowship. God abhorred strongholds, and so they boldly preached freedom to sin-scarred souls.

Modern-Day Holy Discontent Fuel

God *loves* it when his people love what he loves and hate what he hates. He loves it when his followers are disheartened by the things that dishearten him and emboldened by the things he's passionate about. This is the backbone of understanding holy discontent—a simple alliance between God and normal, everyday, earthbound human beings who happen to find themselves stirred up by the *exact* same thing that stirs the heart of the Creator.

In *Holy Discontent*, you read of several leaders whose hearts were stirred up by things that stir the heart of God. On the table below jot down the manifestation of holy discontent that was associated with each person. Let the exercise refresh your belief that God can use a person's holy discontent to change the world for good.

MODERN-DAY HOLY DISCONTENT

Person	Holy Discontent
Martin Luther King Jr. (p. 32)	
Mother Teresa (p. 34)	
Billy Graham (p. 47)	
Bono (p. 102)	

Still today, God involves humankind in his kingdom-building activity through holy discontent: a person sees a problem in the world; God sees the same problem; and together, they resolve to do something about it. Indeed, despite the undeniable challenges involved in ministry leadership, you still find church leaders raising their hands to say yes to tackling the most *unbelievable* problems.

Which of these worthwhile, holy-discontent-fueled challenges (or others you may add to the list) do you see being tackled in your specific ministry setting?

- ❒ Rallying resources for widow and orphan care
- ❒ Caring for single parents
- ❒ Comforting grief-stricken people
- ❒ Breaking strongholds
- ❒ Ending addictive behavior
- ❒ Enfolding lost people in community
- ❒ Establishing partnerships with other churches/ministries
- ❒ Discipling new believers
- ❒ Sending and supporting missionaries
- ❒ Training leaders
- ❒ Working to solve extreme poverty or HIV/AIDS
- ❒ Fighting injustices in the world
- ❒ Serving the needs of people who are underresourced in the community
- ❒ Helping Christ-followers discover and use their spiritual gifts
- ❒ Caring for the sick
- ❒ Releasing artists to use their gifts for God's glory
- ❒ Getting people plugged into small groups
- ❒ Other:

- ❒ Other:

- ❒ Other:

Again, the reason for all this world-changing activity can be boiled down to one idea: people on earth are frustrated by something that's wrong in the world; God is frustrated by the same thing; and together, they determine to do something about it.

Fuel for Your Ministry

I've talked with scores of ministry leaders about the process they went through to find their holy discontent. Based on their input, as well as my own reflection and study, I believe there are three critical questions to ask when trying to locate your holy discontent. They are:

1. What can't you stand?

2. What are you passionate about?

3. What drew you into ministry to begin with?

As you consider your own holy discontent, take this opportunity to evaluate each question in turn.

What Can't You Stand?

Perhaps you have experienced times in your life when something rose up in your spirit and said,

"This is unacceptable!"

"I just can't stand this."

"I can't handle seeing this."

"I refuse just to stand by and watch this unfold."

"This is *not* what God intended."

"I have no category for something like this."

"I don't want to live in a world where this is true."

Maybe you suffered an abuse or a loved one was denied fair treatment or you witnessed extreme poverty for the first time in your life. Maybe you had a meaningful conversation that opened your eyes to injustice or you read a book that expanded your heart to those less fortunate than you or you were given another shot after you had failed miserably. Whatever it was, the experience caused you to feel you might boil over from the sheer frustration you felt toward something in the world that was terribly, terribly wrong.

Here is a sampling of the "firestorm of frustration" experiences leaders have articulated to me:

> "Week in, week out, I was forced to go to a crappy church when I was a kid."

> "I was bullied every single day of ninth grade."

> "I watched footage of the '92 LA riots."

> "My son showed me his photos from a relief trip he took to Rwanda."

> "I saw a homeless man and his young son huddled together in the alley behind my five-bedroom house."

> "I lost my dad to a blood clot that should have been detected."

> "I watched a kid—couldn't have been more than five years old—get beat by his father in the grocery store."

A memory from your childhood, a stirring scene on the evening news, a troubling trend, a challenging relationship, a travesty in another part of the world—these are things that can catalyze firestorms of frustration.

How would you describe your

most memorable ones?

describe

With these situations and experiences in mind, take a moment to complete the sentence starters below.

I can't stand it when . . .

It's unacceptable when . . .

I have no category for . . .

I don't want to live in a world where . . .

Moses couldn't stand oppression and abuse. Mother Teresa couldn't stand extreme poverty. For Martin Luther King Jr. it was racism. For Bono, it is apathy.

Take a look at your conclusions once more, and then distill them down into your own one- or two-word category. Write it in the box below.

distill

What I Can't Stand	

What Are You Passionate About?

Another question to ask when searching for your holy discontent is, *What am I passionate about?* God-given passion pursuits run the gamut; I have met ministry leaders who are passionate about everything from hospital visits to auto maintenance.

Your passion pursuit could be functional families or healthy communications or teaching people how to balance a checkbook. It could be equipping missionaries or organizing teams to encourage them. It could be establishing order in a messy environment or thinking creatively about how to make weekend worship services more inviting.

Think about your leadership role and why you do what you do. What passion pursuits compel you to keep showing up, day after day, to invest your time and energy and creative thought in your area of ministry?

Passion Pursuit   **Why I'm Committed to It**

1. _____   _____

2. _____   _____

3. _____   _____

4. _____   _____

5. _____   _____

What might your passion pursuits tell you about your holy discontent? For example, if you're passionate about healthy communications, think about how God could use that passion to effect positive world change.

If God has placed a drumbeat in your heart for how your contribution can improve this world, then march to it . . . even when nobody else hears it but you!

What First Drew You into Ministry?

For many years my friend Alvin Bibbs served as the director of Extension Ministries at Willow Creek Community Church, helping well-resourced people within the church connect with underresourced men and women in surrounding communities. He is the perfect example of someone who found his holy discontent by considering what first drew him into ministry.

When Bibbs was just a boy, he had the rare opportunity to hear Dr. Martin Luther King Jr. preach live. King spoke about extending love and kindness to one's neighbor, and

> *If God has placed a drumbeat in your heart for how your contribution can improve this world, then march to it . . . even when nobody else hears it but you!*

following the message, young Alvin found himself at the front of the stage, mere inches from Dr. King. The great leader placed hands of blessing on top of young Alvin's head and, in doing so, set Bibbs on a course of ministry that would challenge and inspire him for decades to come. Still today, the powerful memory fuels Bibbs' work on behalf of those who are poor and vulnerable.

Alvin Bibbs was compelled by a vision of equality and justice for every human being, regardless of race, background, or station in life. He got into ministry because he knew God was calling him to make a difference in these arenas.

Consider three more examples of ministry leaders who found their holy discontent by thinking back on why they got involved in ministry to begin with:

- A man who never knew his own dad wound up developing a mentoring program in his local church for young men who need godly male influences.

- A boy grew up watching his mom suffer after losing her husband way too early. The church his family had been part of for more than a decade did nothing to help, and his mom was left feeling forsaken and alone. Now a pastor in a prevailing local church, he has a "whatever it takes" mentality when it comes to supporting their ministry to widows.

- On the heels of an abortion, a teenaged girl was invited to attend a local youth ministry event. The pastor of that group accepted her and put her on a path toward healing and Christlikeness. Today, she's the executive director of a thriving ministry in downtown Chicago that gives financial, employment, and educational opportunities to inner-city young adults. All these years later, she remains totally sold out to providing second chances to every young person she meets.

Thinking back on the starting point of your ministry involvement, how did the influences listed on the chart on the next page factor into your decision to respond to God's call?

WHY I'M INVOLVED IN MINISTRY

Influence on My Calling	When It Occurred and/or Who Was Involved	Why It Was Significant
A meaningful conversation		
An important relationship		
A life-changing experience		
A timely word		
A moment of self-discovery		
A God-given vision		
Other		
Other		

What do your comments on the grid tell you about why you dove into ministry to begin with? (For example, a moment of self-discovery the week before your enrollment papers were due may have caused you to head off to seminary instead of going to a traditional university; from there, your ministry course was set. Or a solid relationship with your dad, who is a pastor, may have propelled you toward church work.) Capture your thoughts below.

What might these responses reveal about your God-given holy discontent? (Perhaps you naturally gravitate toward helping young people in your youth group really think through their goals in life because you experienced the angst of choosing seminary at the very last minute. Or maybe you're a senior pastor who clears the calendar for the dad/son retreat every year, just to have a chance to invest in young men the way your dad invested time and energy with you.) Write your response in the space below.

TAKE ACTION TODAY

Take into account the three primary questions you have answered—*What can't you stand? What are you passionate about?* and *What first drew you into ministry?*

• •

Jot down in the space below how you would sum up what you believe is your God-given holy discontent.

It takes diligent thought to nail down your holy discontent, but it's worth the effort as you learn to leverage the ministry fuel it affords you as a leader. Take action today toward this goal! Keep asking yourself what it is that you can't stand, what it is you're passionate about, and why you first became involved in ministry. Ask God for some insight as you wrestle with those answers. What's more, as you move to chapter 2, "Feed It," take a moment to thank God for the ups, the downs, the interactions and encounters, the successes, the mistakes, the peaks of sheer joy, the valleys of deep despair— all of which he has allowed into your life for a specific purpose, a purpose that he can leverage to change the world, if you will let him!

FEED IT

At the beginning of chapter 1, I made this statement: "The most effective, energetic, motivated, purpose-filled leaders I know are the ones who live and lead from the energy of their holy discontent."

To live and lead from your holy discontent requires first *finding* that holy discontent, which is what you tackled in chapter 1. But in order to leverage it as a limitless fuel source in your ministry, you must also *feed* it. It's not enough to know what you can't stand; leaders realize they also must *do* something about it. In Bishop N. T. Wright's words, "We dream the dream of justice. We glimpse, for a moment, a world at one, a world put to rights, a world where things work out, where societies function fairly and efficiently, where we not only know what we ought to do, but actually *do* it."[3]

THE DESIRE FOR DISTANCE

Admittedly, taking action to put the world to right is a counterintuitive move. In *Holy Discontent*, you read that "the tendency for most of us when we encounter stuff that creates *dis*-ease and frustration in our souls is to push it away. And fast! We feel the discomfort of holy discontentedness coming on, and reflexively we want to medicate it. We want to recoil in disgust at the dreadful realities surrounding us. We want to head to Blockbuster to rent another movie just to stay distanced from it."[4]

And so, as a result:

- The pastor who can't stand seeing people living in cardboard boxes on her own city's streets takes a longer route home every day just to avoid exposing herself to the tragic reality of homelessness.

- The ministry volunteer who grew up suffering unthinkable abuse in a war-torn country refuses to speak of his childhood to *anyone*.

- The leader who lost a son to a meth addiction flips the channel whenever the evening news covers drug-related stories.

Perhaps you can relate. When you consider *your* holy discontent, how have you experienced—in significant or trivial ways—this desire to distance yourself from that which stirs up anger or frustration in you?

For example, once I understood that my holy discontent centered around failing local churches, I faced the very real temptation to hang around only *prevailing* churches. Human nature said,

"If you can't stand to sit in sorry worship services, then don't go!"

"If lifeless pastors make you cringe, then quit spending time with them!"

(Kind of like when you tell your doctor it hurts when you do "this," and he says, "Then don't do *that* anymore!")

Write down your thoughts in the space below.

PRACTICE PROXIMITY

After reading dozens of biblical accounts of strong, successful leaders and drawing some conclusions based on my own empirical observations, this much was clear: The only way to stay energized for the ongoing demands of ministry leadership is to tap into the limitless fuel supply holy discontent provides. And the only way to ensure my holy discontent has any fuel in its reserves is for me to *keep it fed.*

In order to stay fueled for effecting positive change, Moses had to expose himself to the abuse of his people. Martin Luther King Jr. had to get closer to the racial oppression he couldn't stand. Mother Teresa, rather than moving away from it, had to embrace the poverty that wrecked her soul. Bono continues to have to find ways to get face-to-face with apathy wherever he can find it—in the minds of film stars, in the hearts of world leaders, in the eyes of wealthy corporate leaders—in order to help root it out. This is how effective leaders stay revved up, despite the tough stuff of ministry: they move *closer* to that which they can't stand. In short, they practice proximity.

Feeding my holy discontent meant I had to move closer to—*not* farther away from—failing leaders and failing churches. I had to rearrange my leadership role, rearrange my schedule, and, maybe most importantly, rearrange my heart. In fact, I had to be prepared to rearrange *everything* in light of whether my holy discontent was getting fed, or whether it was getting starved.

Weary in Well Doing

Here's how I put it in the book: "Once you find your holy discontent, do whatever you must do to feed it. Again, if it sounds counterintuitive, it's because it is. But as I've often said, the great ongoing danger regarding a person's holy discontent is that its energy will wane. The fuel will dry up. The firestorm will fizzle out. No matter how amped up we are about something that wrecks us, time and repetition take a toll. Another plate of food for a starving orphan, another late-night music rehearsal for an artist, another tutoring class for an inner-city child— if we aren't diligent to feed our holy discontent, we will assuredly become 'weary in well doing' (Galatians 6:9), to borrow a phrase from the apostle Paul."

—Holy Discontent, page 74

What are a few of the realities, dynamics, or people *you* might need to "get closer to" in order to feed your holy discontent?

get close

Gauging One Week's Fuel Supply

A surefire way to tell whether or not you are feeding your holy discontent is to assess how your time and energies are spent. Here's a simple exercise I do at the end of a week, a month, or a ministry season. For this first portion, you'll need your calendar from last week (assuming it was a *work* week, of course; no fair assessing vacation time).

Under the "Accomplishment" column on the next page, note as many completed projects or tasks as you can recall from looking at last week's calendar. Then place a check mark in the "Provided Fuel" column (meaning your energy and optimism actually increased, even if the task was challenging), or the "Drained Fuel" column (meaning your energy declined, even if the task was simple), depending on how you felt after you completed the task. I inserted two examples to get you going.

> "The only way to stay energized for the ongoing demands of ministry leadership is to tap into the limitless fuel supply holy discontent provides. And the only way to ensure my holy discontent has any fuel in its reserves is for me to keep it fed."

IMPACT FROM MY WEEK'S ACCOMPLISHMENTS

Accomplishment	Provided Fuel	Drained Fuel
x. Counseled a senior staff member who was frustrated by a misunderstanding within his team		✓
x. Gave a talk to help another church kick off their three-year capital campaign	✓	

FEEDit

Review your completed chart on page 37 to see what strikes you as interesting or unusual. For example, did you find that something you enjoy about your role actually drained fuel from you? Or, on the flip side of that coin, did you discover that the weekly leadership team meeting you never seem to have time for provided fuel to face the week's demands? Note your observations in the space below.

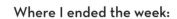

Doing this exercise always gives me a pretty clear picture of where my fuel supply stands. Based on the information recorded on your chart, you should also be able to see the overall impact on your ministry leadership fuel supply for the week you assessed.

How much energy or fuel for ministry work did you feel you had when you went into the week, and how fueled or energized were you at week's end? Draw a horizontal line on each gauge below to represent both levels.

MY WEEK'S FUEL SUPPLY: BEFORE AND AFTER

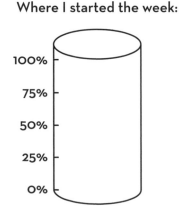

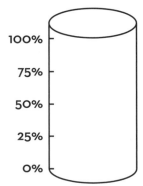

assess

If feeling fueled has a direct correlation to feeding holy discontent, then what do your fuel readings tell you about how well your holy discontent got fed during the week you assessed?

Gauging Fuel Supply for a Ministry Season

Now that you know how the exercise works, try expanding the parameters. Think back on the past season of your ministry journey. If you just came off of Christmas, then your "season" may include the weeks or months of preparation all the way up to Christmas Eve. If it's still early in the calendar year, you might evaluate the last twelve months of your ministry. If you've just wrapped up a multi-year capital campaign, then perhaps that's the "season" you want to evaluate. On the chart on the following page, write down the season of ministry and several of your completed tasks. Then designate with check marks whether the completed task filled or drained your fuel tank.

Example:

January–December, Last Year
Ministry Season

Accomplishment	Provided Fuel	Drained Fuel
Trip to minister to churches in India		✓
Monthly elder meetings to finalize Willow's strategic plan	✓	

IMPACT OF MY MINISTRY SEASON

Ministry Season

Accomplishment	Provided Fuel	Drained Fuel

Review the check marks you placed in the "Provided Fuel" column. Circle the percentage below that reflects how much of your time was spent engaging in tasks that fueled you:

Percentage of Completed Tasks that Fueled You	What Might Be True for You
About **10%**	I've obviously had a tough run recently. In fact, it seems almost nothing about my role has been adding to my fuel level.
About **25%**	For one reason or another, only about a quarter of what I was responsible for actually fueled me during the past year.
About **50%**	I'd say half of what I accomplished provided at least a little energy boost.
About **75%**	Better than half of all that I did in ministry leadership over the past twelve months fueled me.
Almost **100%**	I'm thriving these days! Nearly everything I touch gives me greater energy, optimism, and stamina for the road ahead.

articulate

Take a look at the statement listed beside the percentage you circled. Is it true for you? How else would you articulate the state of affairs in your ministry right now?

Keep these thoughts in mind as you move ahead.

READ THE GAUGES

I've noticed that some leaders are able to perform this type of assessment intuitively—and on a moment-by-moment basis. For me, though, I have to pull away every once in a while and actually lay it all out, as you've just done. Going through the paces in this way always proves beneficial as I work to stay fueled for the ministry road ahead. I think you too will benefit from your diligence to scrutinize the way your ministry tasks *really* affect you.

Let me give you two learnings or "ahas" I made one time when I completed a similar grid and "read the gauges" after what had been a really rigorous ministry season.

Aha 1: I was surprised to discover that our monthly elder board meetings were extremely fueling to me. These are six-hour marathon meetings that are stuffed full of complex and challenging problems to solve. Everything on the agenda represents a major issue affecting lots of people and lots of money. Still, I consistently found myself leaving those meetings begging for more! Each time, I could have stayed all night if it meant sinking my teeth into one more solution-seeking discussion to help Willow get better.

Aha 2: I was struck by the fact that, although I feel called and equipped to do work with churches in other countries, the travel itself was a huge drain for me. But if I'm called to global ministry and equipped for global ministry, then shouldn't global ministry *provide* fuel for me? After a lot of thought and prayer, I found my answer: I needed to more closely link the motivation behind these trips to my holy discontent, lest the logistics and complexities of international travel utterly wipe me out. Once I added the parameter that every international trip I take must be *directly* related to establishing leadership training programs for local church pastors in that country, my fuel tank bubbled over. I had to see plainly that my efforts were tied to my holy discontent of helping local churches—and local church leaders—to get better.

See what "ahas" you can uncover as you take another look at your expanded "Ministry Season" chart on page 40. Answer the following questions in the space that follows each.

WHAT TYPES OF ACTIVITIES OR INTERACTIONS INCREASE YOUR FUEL SUPPLY?

Activities that increase my fuel supply include . . .

Interactions that increase my fuel supply include . . .

WHAT TYPES OF ACTIVITIES OR INTERACTIONS DECREASE YOUR FUEL SUPPLY?

Activities that decrease my fuel supply include . . .

Interactions that decrease my fuel supply include . . .

MAKE NECESSARY CHANGES

Feeding your holy discontent takes creative maneuvering. Systems have to shift. Priorities have to shift. Attitudes and expectations have to shift. (Ask me how I know.) But the end result is the topped-off fuel source you keep reading about, which equates to a heck of a lot more abundance episodes for you as a ministry leader. More episodes of realized grace. More episodes of realized peace. More episodes of realized rest. More *abundance*, through and through.

Dream On

Consider this: If you were to go all out in feeding your holy discontent in your current leadership role, which of your involvements and interactions might need to change? For instance, if your holy discontent deals with ministering to homeless people in your city, but you can't break out of your weekly routine to actually get to the shelter, then your standing appointments might need to shift.

Spend a few moments dreaming about what your ministry life would look like if you got serious about feeding your holy discontent. On the chart on pages 45–46, jot down ideas for changes that would need to occur; then provide a couple of numeric rankings in the second and third columns. First, on a scale of 1 to 5 (1 being "low impact" and 5 being "high impact"), gauge the impact each change would have on getting your holy discontent fed. Next, on a scale of 1 to 5 (1 being "unlikely" and 5 being "very likely"), gauge the likelihood that you would actually commit to the change in your current leadership situation.

> *Feeding your holy discontent takes creative maneuvering. Systems have to shift. Priorities have to shift. Attitudes and expectations have to shift. (Ask me how I know.) But the end result is the topped-off fuel source you keep reading about, which equates to a heck of a lot more abundance episodes for you as a ministry leader.*

CHANGES TO BE MADE

Changes I Must Make to Feed Holy Discontent	Impact of the Change 1 2 3 4 5 low high	Likelihood I'll Commit to Making It 1 2 3 4 5 unlikely very likely
ATTITUDES/ASSUMPTIONS Am I grateful for my holy discontent? Am I pessimistic about people understanding why I do what I do? What changes to my thought patterns would help to feed my holy discontent?		
LEADERSHIP STYLE ISSUES AND HABITS Do I close myself off from the people I lead or serve? Do I manage from a distance? What changes to the way I lead would help to feed my holy discontent?		
STANDING APPOINTMENTS AND MEETINGS Have I allowed my calendar to crowd out any hope for engaging in holy-discontent-feeding opportunities? What changes to my routine would free me up to do so?		
RELATIONSHIPS Who fuels my holy discontent and who steals my joy? What changes to my circle of influence would help feed my holy discontent?		

continued

CHANGES TO BE MADE

Changes I Must Make to Feed Holy Discontent	Impact of the Change 1 2 3 4 5 low high	Likelihood I'll Commit to Making It 1 2 3 4 5 unlikely very likely
PRIORITIES Am I prone to dismissing tasks that would fuel my holy discontent in favor of tending to things I feel I "should" do instead? What changes to the way I prioritize my activity would help to feed my holy discontent?		
OTHER INVOLVEMENTS What other changes to my tasks and responsibilities would help to feed my holy discontent?		
OTHER INTERACTIONS What other changes to my relational world would help to feed my holy discontent?		

Overcome Obstacles, Stifle Fears

Check your completed chart to see if any items ranked "high" on the impact scale but "low" on the likelihood scale. What obstacles or fears, real or perceived, caused you to rank these necessary changes as "low" on the likelihood scale?

Change:

Why you ranked it "low likelihood":

Change:

Why you ranked it "low likelihood":

Change:

Why you ranked it "low likelihood":

Forsaking Power to Feed Holy Discontent: Jane Overstreet's Story

Jane Overstreet is a leader who understands well what it means to see a few raised eyebrows as a result of pursuing God-given holy discontent. As a lawyer for a worldwide ministry, she possessed enormous influence and credibility among her colleagues. It was a job everyone considered "ideal"— including her. But over time, she began to notice a terrible trend: the international missions organizations and ministry leaders she interacted with lacked leadership and strategic-thinking skills. As a result, they often made poor decisions that under-mined their ability to effectively meet the needs of the people they set out to serve. And because these leaders lived in some of the most inaccessible, underresourced places in the world, help wasn't exactly on the way.

Overstreet left her legal profession in order to rally a few associates around the vision of training and developing

continued next page

Which of the changes you noted are you most motivated to overcome? Place a star beside it and hang onto that thought as you move ahead. Keep in mind that, although there is no magic bullet for overcoming the obstacles and stifling the fears that relate to feeding your holy discontent, when you find yourself stymied, it always helps to look to the One who was pulled in a million directions and yet never once veered off course. If ever there was a person who knew his "one thing" and stayed perfectly on purpose every day of his ministry, it was Jesus Christ.

Don't Lose the Plot

Jesus knew that the sole reason he was sent by God to planet Earth was to testify to the truth. Even so, he could have wrapped himself around easier, lower impact endeavors like parking lot expansions or mission trip bake sales or increased "What Would *I* Do?" market penetration. He could have blown all his time on lesser visions, instead of pursuing the *one thing* God explicitly had asked him to do. Like so many pastors and leaders who have been talked out of their holy discontent by more vocal pressures and obligations, he could have lost the plot.

But Jesus *didn't* lose the God-given plot that had been written for his specific ministry—the ministry he was called to, equipped for, and sanctioned to do. And please hear me on this: even when the stakes are high and the pressure's on, neither can you.

Read Jane Overstreet's story (left), paying special attention to the last couple of lines. Friend, you too have the opportunity to be "obedient to the thing you are called to do." But like many ministry leaders, maybe you think the risks are too great or the obstacles are too insurmountable for you to feed your holy discontent.

How easy or difficult would it be for you to "stay put" regarding your leadership role instead of endeavoring to make some holy-discontent-feeding changes? Rate yourself by placing an "X" on the scale below.

easy 1 2 3 4 5 6 7 8 9 difficult

You may think it will be *far* easier just to keep doing what you're doing (who will know the difference, right?), even if what you're doing isn't working all that well for you. I've certainly found myself in that thought pattern before. But the thought that stops the stagnancy every time is that one day, I will find myself standing before God—with Jesus Christ right by his side, mind you . . . you know, the One who *refused* to neglect his holy discontent. Somehow, I just can't imagine trying to explain why I couldn't pull away from other responsibilities in order to pursue the "one thing" God has asked for me to do!

Someday, we *both* will stand before Jesus, who did not lose the plot regarding why God called him into ministry. We will be asked to give an account for how wisely we served his Bride, the church. We will be asked to tell how well we "led with all diligence." We will be asked what we did about that one thing—the primary firestorm of frustration—God placed in our hearts.

Personally, I can't imagine looking into the eyes of Christ and admitting that—despite the presence of the Holy Spirit, the availability of rest and peace and abundance, and the fantastic leadership development resources all around me—the whole ministry leadership thing just kind of got away from me. My guess is that you can't imagine doing that either, so let's get working on the task of feeding holy discontent. Deal?

effective ministry leaders. She and her team set out to teach these ministry leaders practical ways to tackle things like strategic planning, financial management, even team building. The move required her to forsake the positional power she'd enjoyed all those years, but fighting for a worthy cause scratches an even deeper itch for Jane: "Risks like the one I took require you to be honest about the price of leadership. It's not for everyone, but as far as I'm concerned, creating room for the Holy Spirit to *radically* change leaders . . . watching them become freed up to use their gifts for the sake of kingdom good . . . *this* is what gets me up in the morning and keeps me lighted up all day."

In the end, Jane Overstreet traded in *her idea* for *God's ideal*. And she did it for one reason alone: her holy discontent *demanded* to be fed. "The most valuable thing you can do in this life is to be obedient to the thing you are called to do," Jane says. "It's the highest value I know."

GET GOING!

If you need permission to make some critical changes in order to feed your holy discontent, it is hereby granted! Make no apologies for living from the cutting edge and limitless energy of your holy discontent. Let it guide you in your day-to-day leadership role: in doing so, you will honor God's plan, leverage Christ's power, and relieve the soulish ache for *impact* that every leader senses.

So where should you begin? Keep in mind that, although the by-products of well-fed holy discontent are absolutely ingenious, the process itself is not rocket science. It simply requires openness to what God wishes to do in and through you in order to fix what is broken in this world. Take a look at the list below, placing a check mark beside ideas that might serve your holy discontent well.

☐ READ A BOOK

Once you have completed your "required reading" each week, there is often no time or energy left to read something that speaks to a more intimate side of you. This is especially true for teaching pastors who must frequently prepare talks; they complete the research portion of their role and are so weary of staring at words on a page that they neglect this fundamental means of feeding holy discontent.

Don't let this be true for you! Even if your investment equals fifteen minutes a day, be sure to pick up the colorful, life-changing distinctions that only come by reading people who are wiser, more advanced, more articulate, and more traveled than you.

☐ TAKE A TRIP

When is the last time you traveled for a reason other than vacation? Consider inserting yourself into a brand-new culture for the simple sake of exposing your heart, expanding your horizons, and enriching your soul. Who knows what God might do on such a trip?

❏ GET INVOLVED

The tendency for ministry leaders is to be aware only of their purview of responsibility. This happens both at the senior pastor level (they know what's being preached in weekend services but never knew their church offered a quarterly abuse recovery workshop) and at the departmental level (they know all about the games planned for the student retreat next weekend but can't seem to recall the church's overall vision).

Ask questions of your leaders and staff and peers. Discover opportunities for growth and development that may feed your holy discontent, and then *seize* them! If you are a pastor with teenagers at home and you want to understand their world, then show up at a students' retreat. You might just learn something . . . and feed your holy discontent while you're at it. If you're an arts leader who suffered abuse somewhere along the way, drop in on a planning meeting the pastoral care department is doing for the abuse recovery workshop. Ask what you can do to help. You never know where a step like that might lead!

❏ HAVE A CONVERSATION

Seek out a few people who can relate to your holy discontent, and test your inclinations for feeding your holy discontent with them. Ask them a few of the questions you've been asked to address in this companion guide, such as:

What catalysts drove your passion pursuits?

When did you know that God was asking you to be part of the solution on this issue?

What are you reading these days?

Where are you serving?

How are you maintaining balance between your current responsibilities and the emerging desires of your heart?

Your genuine interest will honor the other person, as well as help you to gather a few hints about how to manage your own holy discontent.

Forsaking Comfort to Feed Holy Discontent: Doug Sparks's Story

Doug Sparks is a pastor in western Colorado whose family recently moved back to the States after having lived abroad for more than two decades. "My three children are all postmoderns," Spark's explains. "Within a few short years of our return, I remember standing on the shore, figuratively speaking, watching helplessly as the riptide of modern culture swept them into a world that was far from mine."

In collaboration with other creative leaders, he put together an edgy and spontaneous weekly meeting (branded as "A Postmodern Whatever") on his church's campus that serves as a "safe environment where twenty-somethings' questions, concerns, and ideas are received seriously, respectfully, and without judgment." Doug had a choice: either succumb to the waves that were washing over his kids or wade right into the water. Feeling resolute, albeit totally ill-equipped, he dove in and started swimming. According to him, his journey into his kids' world left a trail of tears in his wake, but along the way, he made a wonderful discovery: "I found their generation to be truly lost—literally . . . they have zero reference points—but at the same time, truly *caring*. They desperately want to be challenged, they want to make a difference that is not overshadowed

continued on page 54

☐ LOOK AROUND YOU!

One of my favorite ways to feed my own holy discontent is just to get my eyes off my own deal and take a look around. Sometimes, the opportunities for leveraging holy discontent in the world around us are so obvious that, if we're not careful, we'll miss them altogether. Take a look at Pastor Doug Sparks' story (left) for a perfect example of someone who *didn't* miss his opportunity to feed his holy discontent.

There are as many ways to feed holy discontent as there are creative minds to dream them up. Let the aforementioned suggestions serve as a starting point for you, but don't let it limit your activity. Take another look at the ideas you placed check marks beside. Based on those ideas, as well as action items you would like to add, jot down the practical steps you can take to begin feeding your holy discontent and the timeframe in which you will take those steps on the chart on page 53.

FEEDING MY HOLY DISCONTENT

Steps I'll Take to Ensure My Holy Discontent Gets Fed	When I Commit to Taking Them

by the achievement of their parents' generation, and they want, most of all, to experience personal freedom."

He and his wife concluded twenty years of service on the mission field, having no idea the next era of their lives would involve local church ministry. But it's a tide he can't not splash around in, this compelling desire to help postmoderns learn how to ask thoughtful questions, challenge the assumptions that crop into their consciousness, and seek ultimate truth. "The format each week resembles a crap shoot more than a carefully crafted production," he admits, "but we would much rather leave these young women and men with a dozen really good questions than one really rehearsed answer."

The task of becoming a fellow pilgrim to a bunch of men and women half his age who need to know the all-perfect, all-loving, all-accepting, full-of-grace God he knows is a challenging one. But once his frustration over the distance he sensed between him and his children had reached fever pitch, nothing could have kept him out of those waves.

Doug Sparks was crystal clear about his holy discontent: he couldn't stand to see his kids swept up in a cultural system he didn't endorse. But he had to look up from the comfort and convenience of his routine and take a look around in order to see the glaring opportunity to feed his holy discontent staring right back at him, plain as day.

SPEAK IT OUT

An action item every leader needs to take to feed their holy discontent is simply to *speak it out*. Start by talking about your holy discontent with the people you serve and lead, and see what God will do through you as you open new windows of insight into your life and leadership for people who serve alongside you.

Author Dan Allender, founder and president of Mars Hill Graduate School, says that "a leader—whether in the home, church, business, community, or government—has authority due to her role, but her positional power will not bring about good for individuals or organizations unless it is backed up by the capital of character. You may obey a leader who has power and authority, but you will not strive to serve her or the cause of the organization unless you *respect* and *care for her*."[5]

And yet how will a person "respect and care for" you unless they really know you? God has wired you up with a specific mission that is custom-fitted to *your* gift mix, *your* interests, *your* geographical locale, *your* experience base, *your* idiosyncrasies, even. Squelching your holy discontent in a wild attempt to be that which other people *need you to be*, instead of that which you *are*, will throw your life and the lives of those you lead into sheer turmoil.

Because leaders often seem not only *unknown* but also *unknowable* to those they lead, one of the greatest gifts you can give your team is to come out of hiding and speak openly about your holy discontent.

One of the teaching pastors at Willow Creek has a holy discontent that revolves around letting people know that God loves them and wants desperately to relate with them in an intimate way. Like Billy Graham, he just *can't stand* for people to meander through life, having no idea there is a God who cares.

This pastor was already teaching during weekend services at Willow with a high degree of frequency, but his holy discontent demanded more. He made his need known to the rest of the teaching team, and together we landed on a fantastic solution that would honor God, satisfy this pastor's "need to feed," and serve our broader church family really well. Willow partners with a local church in a nearby suburb, and they frequently need people to come teach so that they can give their regular pastors and teachers a break. Guess who was the perfect fit for filling those slots?

I trace this whole solution back to one decision made by one pastor in one local church: he decided to *speak*. He told his fellow leaders about his soul-level holy discontent and then sought out ways to feed it. Talk about a God-glorifying move!

Try this experiment, if you dare: for the next seven days, give voice to your holy discontent *each and every* day. For one week's time, speak it out. Put words to it. Incorporate it into conversation with your direct reports, your boss, your volunteer teams, and your ministry partners.

> *Squelching your holy discontent in a wild attempt to be that which other people need you to be, instead of that which you are, will throw your life and the lives of those you lead into sheer turmoil.*

Give the following statements a test run with other leaders you trust; or, if these feel unnatural to you, write in additional statements that gel with your personality and style.

These days my heart is really drawn toward _____.
How does that line up with who you know me to be?

I'm becoming more and more interested in_____.
If you come across any good resources or opportunities that would be a fit, I'd love to hear about them.

I don't really know where all of this is leading or what it all means yet, but lately I have a growing concern for _____.

I've been wondering recently if God gave me the intense frustration I've been feeling regarding _____.
What do you know about this issue?

Once you begin to talk about your holy discontent, resources you never imagined might just open up to you. Promise me this: as the divine "feeding" opportunities cross your desk, seize them!

DITCH SECRET-AGENT STATUS

Allow me a final note regarding this issue of speaking out your holy discontent. One of the biggest fears I see plaguing ministry leaders is the fear that if they feed their holy discontent by wrapping more and more of their formal role around it, people (elders, pastors, staff members, family members, friends, whoever) will think they're shirking duties in their "real" job. They live with the perpetual fear that the pursuit of their holy discontent may not sit well with the people around them.

So the ministry leader with a missional mindset passes up the trip with her church's relief team that is headed to New Orleans and in doing so drips a little more water on her firestorm of frustration. The senior pastor (from chapter 1, as you'll recall) who is on fire about incorporating the arts in weekend worship services but skips another planning meeting in order to do a hospital visit stamps out his flame too. In essence, they live as holy discontent secret agents who go on about their ministry lives suppressing that which is *most true* and *most real* of themselves.

It's a status that must get extremely exhausting, if you ask me. I've seen one too many ministry leaders refuse to acknowledge and feed their God-given holy discontent and invest themselves in *escaping* from ministry instead. They have to find some way to compensate for the coping energy exerted to keep who they *really* are under wraps, and so they numb their areas of passion, trudge through yet another ministry season, and count down the days until summer vacation.

As a leader, you must make a choice: either squelch your holy discontent, or take the risk to let it be known. You know my vote: only the latter option enables you to live and lead from your holy discontent.

I don't know about you, but I for one am not interested in living in a world untouched by holy-discontented heroes like Moses and Mother Teresa and Martin Luther King Jr. and Bono. Just think what we'd all be like if we had no feelings of outrage toward abuse, no sensitivity toward the poor, no appreciation for racial equality, no disdain for treatable or curable disease, and so forth.

The stakes of starved holy discontent are ridiculously high, not only for these heroes, but also for you. God crafted you to reflect his character and called you into ministry leadership to effect necessary change in a very broken world. Don't let yourself be counted among those who refuse to feed their holy discontent and, in so doing, deny the world of the "one thing" you have to offer it!

When I consider what could transpire if *every* leader in *every* church was fully dedicated to living from the energy of his or her unique, holy discontent passion, the potential impact is simply mind-blowing. God has built you for a purpose that will serve your generation effectively, my friend. Now, your role is to live and lead from it . . . no apologies.

Part II

INVIGORATE
Holy Discontent in Those You Lead

3

CHOOSE THE FUNDAMENTAL STATE

A movie named *Alexander* came out a few years ago that portrayed the meteoric rise of a twenty-five-year-old warrior in ancient Greece around 300 BC. After leading a triumphant campaign northward, defeating every foe who tried to stand between him and victory, Alexander wound up becoming king of the known world.

There's a great scene in the film in which Alexander's army, which is Macedonian, is about to take on the far more numerous Persian troops, who are fighting on behalf of the mightiest empire in existence. Alexander gets on his horse, rides to the front of the battle line, and trots back and forth as he eyes the guys who are about to go into battle with him.

"Today, we ride to our destiny!" he says, to the sound of raucous cheers. He stops in front of one soldier, calls him by name, and says, "How far was it you threw your man wrestling at the last Olympic games? Will you match your strength with your spirit today?"

The crowd erupts in laughter and cheers as the fighter gives Alexander a resounding "Yes!"

The leader moves farther down the line and calls another of his soldiers by name. "You are the son of a man who was a great soldier to my father. I still mourn your brother who died so bravely as well . . . what an honored family you descend from! You will fight for *them* today." Alexander puts his fist over his heart as he stares at the soldier from atop his horse.

He proceeds down the line, stopping every so often to acknowledge yet another soldier's reason for being so fired up about giving the Persians a pounding that day. I got the feeling as I looked at the faces of the tens of thousands who stood behind that front line that Alexander could have singled out every last one of his men and recounted why it was each one was fighting for the glory of Greece. It is a perfect image of what it means to help others live and lead from their holy discontent.

Not only was Alexander clear about his own holy discontent (for more on that, you'll have to rent the movie), but he knew the holy discontent of the people he led. When it was time to take the next hill, he knew precisely how to draw out their individual passion and rev them up for victory.

In chapters 1 and 2, you learned how to find and feed your own holy discontent. In this chapter and in chapter 4, you'll learn how to identify and help feed holy discontent in those you lead. Once your entire team is living and leading from holy discontent, *you'll* take the next hill with confidence and energy too.

For starters, what "hill" or major undertaking are you and those you lead or serve preparing for right now? How confident are you that you will achieve your objective? (For example, one of the biggest initiatives on my radar right now is the implementation of Willow's new strategic plan. I'm very confident we'll achieve our stated objectives because some very smart, very talented folks have been working hard on this. Still, I've endured my share of sleepless nights over this one!) Write about your biggest hill in the space below.

Romans 12:8 says that we are to take our leadership hills *diligently*. The original Greek word for diligence, *spoudé*, speaks of things like eagerness and earnestness and *care*. Which pretty much means you can neither steamroll nor remain distanced from those you lead and still adhere to this biblical mandate. When the Bible calls pastors and leaders to lead with all diligence, then in part it's calling us to *care for those we lead*. And one of the most caring expressions you can give them is to help them find and feed their holy discontent. It's how they too can tap into that extra energy supply you discovered in Part I.

Whether you are feeling Alexanderlike as you face your hill, or you are struggling just to stay on your horse, this chapter holds great promise for you. I know this, because we *all* can stand to get a little bit better in caring for those we lead and serve.

When you help the ones you lead find their holy discontent—and then feed it—the end result is significant: people feel *known*, *valued*, and *supported* in the distinct ways they contribute to the overall mission. Over time, you'll build a culture of leadership diligence, of *spoudé*-style care, in which every contributor operates from a bottomless supply of passion-fueled energy.

To create this culture, leaders must make three choices. They must choose to:

1. Enter the fundamental state of leadership.

2. Help find the holy discontent of those they lead and serve.

3. Provide those they lead and serve with ways to feed that holy discontent.

We'll explore the first choice in this chapter and the next two choices in chapter 4.

> When you help the ones you lead find their holy discontent—and then feed it—the end result is spectacular: people feel known, valued, and supported in the distinct ways they contribute to the overall mission.

UNDERSTANDING STATES OF LEADERSHIP

If you apply heat to an ice cube, it turns to water. In other words, it changes states. And if you apply heat to that water, then it changes states yet again: this time, from water to steam. Here's why I bring this up: what is true for ice cubes is also true for leaders.

As a ministry leader, you always exist in a "state"—one state when you're soaring, thriving, and getting things done; another state when you're struggling, wrestling, and begging for relief; and some state in between when you're just getting by. But here is the intriguing part: if you "heat up" your holy discontent—by finding it, feeding it, staying close to it, and speaking it out—then, just like the ice cube, you too can change states. The realities of who you are and the circumstances you face don't change, but your ability to face them, accurately size them up, and effect change in them does.

How does the notion that you can change your leadership state at will strike you? Note how you would assess yourself on the continuum below.

As a ministry leader, I have tended to believe that . . .

The way I lead is a fixed value; it's just "who I am"

The way I lead is a fluid value that shifts or morphs depending on the decisions I make

You will explore your ability to change leadership states in a later section, but first, let's define the two primary states we're talking about, the "normal" state and the "fundamental" state.

The Normal State

At some point, every leader (myself included) operates from the place known as the "normal" state. The normal state is the place that reflects the fallen nature that has characterized humankind since the days of Adam and Eve and is marked by dynamics like self-interest, scarcity thinking, ambiguity, and routine. But perhaps the most unfortunate thing about the normal state is that it's a leader's *default position*.

Here is how you'll know when you're operating in the normal state:

- You feel unusually overwhelmed by your usual workload.

- Your concerns are mostly self-focused.

- Your ego gets in the way of the cause.

- You lead out of obligation or compulsion.

- Your leadership vision seems fuzzy.

- You wonder if you can impact the current state of affairs.

- You are reactive rather than proactive when making decisions.

- You'd rather maintain the status quo than risk kicking up dust by making changes.

Let me give you an example of how the normal state gets played out. I have a friend who is a senior pastor of a large urban church. He is a strong person and a fantastic leader, but he wrestles with his pride. A few years ago, he experienced what the normal state was all about—specifically the part about ego getting in the way of the cause—when his church decided to shift to multisite ministry.

For weeks, local media trumpeted his innovative leadership and the church's interesting approach to expansion. Later, he admitted that somewhere along the way, he began to crave the praise.

The church faced some significant strategy and timing decisions in the months leading up to launch, but rather than relying on his senior leadership team for direction, this pastor plowed ahead in his own way and at his own hasty pace.

> *In the normal state, lots of things suffer: your ability to generate creative solutions, your ability to sustain organizational momentum or team unity, and your ability to sense the Holy Spirit's direction in your life.*

Today, he reflects on that season of his leadership with embarrassment. "I completely lost the plot and treated my team like they were nothing more than an annoyance to me. I thought I was justified in sidelining them, because from my point of view, they were serving only to stand in the way of 'my deal' getting done."

His end game may have been laudable—to launch more ministry venues and expose more people to God's message—but his steamroll method was costly. Because he let his ego lead, he experienced that strange sensation leaders often feel of charging ahead, only to turn around and realize that nobody is following. Talk about a blow to team unity! It was a humbling experience, to say the least.

In the normal state, lots of things suffer: your ability to generate creative solutions, your ability to sustain organizational momentum or team unity, your ability to sense the Holy Spirit's direction in your life, and so forth.

Take a moment to review the normal state descriptions on page 65. Use the chart on page 67 to work through these questions:

- When you think about the ebb and flow of your leadership effectiveness, which of the listed descriptions have you experienced?

- What suffered in the wake of your normal-state behavior?

- What did you learn as a result?

MY VENTURES INTO THE NORMAL STATE

	The "Normal" State Behavior I Exhibited	What Suffered as a Result	What I Learned
x.	Ego got in the way of the cause	Team unity	Humility

CHOOSEit

Remember, the normal state is called "normal" for a reason. If you are there right now, you're assuredly not alone. In fact, at one time or another, every leader I know faces the challenging reality of trying to lead while tangled up in a normal state of existence.

I was introduced to this idea of the normal state by author and business school professor Robert Quinn. He says, "When we accept the world as it is, we deny our ability to see something better, and hence our ability to *be* something better. We become what we behold."[6] Truly, the normal state is a terrible place to be. It's sparse. It's stifling. And it eats hope for breakfast. No leader worth her compensation wants to lead from a posture marked by self-consumption, ego, obligation, insecurity, or reactivity. What a relief it is, then, to know that another option exists.

The Fundamental State

In his book *Building the Bridge as You Walk on It*, Professor Quinn says, "Most of us spend our time unconsciously colluding in our own diminishment and the diminishment of the organization."[7] In other words, we unconsciously settle for the normal state. We neglect to dream big dreams, for ourselves and for our ministries.

After studying hundreds of leaders in dozens of leadership settings, however, Quinn made an interesting observation. When a leader was gripped by a powerful passion (a "holy discontent") and was tuned into how that passion could provide fuel for leadership challenges, the leader actually entered a *different state of mind*. Quinn called his discovery the "fundamental state theory," and it proves itself out each time a leader makes a decision to leave behind self-centeredness and scarcity thinking and instead chooses to lead from the place where enthusiasm, persistence, and group-desired results reign supreme.

I watched this happen with an arts team that was rehearsing for a drama we planned to use in an Easter service one year. Tensions rose as actors dropped lines, technicians missed lighting cues, and the culminating scene of the entire sketch fell flat. The producer called a fifteen-minute break, and when they reconvened, she asked everyone to push Pause on the issues that were plaguing the rehearsal and instead tap back into the original passion for the sketch.

> When a leader was gripped by a powerful passion (a "holy discontent") and was tuned into how that passion could provide fuel for leadership challenges, the leader actually entered a different state of mind.

"For a few minutes here, I want you to forget about your tasks related to pulling this off and instead get back to your passion associated with it. Why did you sign up for this drama to begin with?" she asked.

Every single team member had a friend or a family member who was living far from God and who would be attending one of the Easter services that weekend. As soon they tapped back into their original motivation—helping point all those folks toward God—the rehearsal went smoothly. The reality of their circumstances didn't shift, but their ability to effect change did.

For our purposes, consider that Quinn's fundamental state represents *living and leading from holy discontent*, and that his normal state, where you accept the world as it is, represents *not living and leading from holy discontent.*

FUNDAMENTAL STATE = Living and leading from holy discontent

NORMAL STATE = *Not* living and leading from holy discontent

Take a look at how the two states contrast each other on the chart below:

THE TWO STATES OF LEADERSHIP

The Normal State	The Fundamental State
You feel *unusually* overwhelmed by your *usual* workload.	You possess a deep reservoir of enthusiasm and energy.
Your concerns are mostly self-focused.	You concentrate on the needs of the mission and those fighting for it.
Your ego gets in the way of the cause.	You lead with a surrendered ego.
You lead out of obligation or compulsion.	You lead from your original passion.
Your leadership vision seems fuzzy.	You experience clarity of vision.
You wonder if you can impact the current state of affairs.	You are willing to take risks.
Your decision-making stance becomes reactive.	You are confident, especially regarding decision making.
You'd rather maintain the status quo than risk effecting change.	You're open to change, if it means taking ground for the cause.

Take a close look at the "Fundamental State" column on page 69. Even if you haven't had the language to name it, you've most likely experienced it. In the space below, describe what it feels like to lead from the fundamental state—the leadership state marked by enthusiasm and energy, a surrendered ego, risk tolerance, confidence, and so forth.

Which one of the fundamental-state dynamics, such as high energy, confidence, openness to change, etc.—have you experienced in your ministry leadership role most recently? What were the circumstances surrounding the episode? Jot down your thoughts below.

Quinn says that leaders who step into the fundamental state—even momentarily—shift mental gears altogether and begin to operate on an entirely new level. I've seen it happen time and time again in our worship service planning meetings. The team will fall into a creative rut, but then one of us will say, "Okay, it's time for a blue-sky discussion. For the next twenty-five minutes, I want our best collective thinking on this topic. Dream big! No idea is bad. No restrictions or limitations are valid. Nothing but blue skies ahead, agreed? Go!"

The exercise is effective because it gives every participant permission to put the pressures of the day aside and tap back into their original passion for ministry.

Undoubtedly, when the twenty-five minutes is up, the vibe of the room has shifted. Where there was exhaustion there is now energy. Where there was fear there is now confidence. Where there was an attachment to the status quo there is now risk tolerance. And inevitably, albeit using different words, one of us will acknowledge how great it feels to be back in the fundamental state.

Whenever you experience a fundamental-state episode, mark the occasion and relish the buzz! Over time, you'll train yourself to enter the fundamental state with greater and greater frequency. This is important because it is only when you operate from the fundamental state that you do ministry from a place of *passion*—the powerful, inspiring foundation of your holy discontent. And it is your holy discontent that aligns you with God's plan to usher in a new reality marked by energy, clarity, selflessness, and hope.

You would think that we'd all take up permanent residence in the fundamental state, given how terrific it is to operate there. But in my own leadership, as well as in the lives of the leaders I mentor, I notice a troubling trend. Despite how great the fundamental state seems, our tendency is to resist it, rather than to embrace it.

Can you relate to this dynamic? Why might it be easier to remain in the normal state instead of stepping into the fundamental state? Check whichever statements are true for you.

The normal state:

☐ Requires less energy

☐ Feels safer

☐ Doesn't call for unnecessary risk

☐ Affords me time to "process"

☐ Preserves a manageable pace of change

☐ Doesn't force decisive action

☐ Allows for ambiguity regarding an emerging vision

☐ Protects my pride

If you find yourself firmly planted in the normal state (and frustrated that you're there), then be reminded that in this chapter we are exploring our ability to make a *choice* for change. Keep reading to discover how to do just that.

CHANGING YOUR STATE OF LEADERSHIP

In *Holy Discontent* I describe a meeting I attended with "big dog" leaders from a whole host of sectors—academia, government, business, not-for-profit organizations—dealing with alleviating HIV/AIDS in Africa.[8] Although many people seated around the table didn't know each other prior to the meeting, once we'd heard each one describe his or her holy discontent, collectively we chose to step into the fundamental state.

Everyone around the table was a high-profile leader with a lot of influence and a lot of power. And yet there was not a single power play made. Truly, the members of that little discussion decided to care more about creating a shared result than about getting their way.

When I had time later to reflect on the meeting, I realized that the decision to leave the normal state and enter the fundamental state required nothing supernatural, magical, or mystical. Instead, all it took was a simple invitation. As the meeting began, I posed this question: "As it pertains to solving the HIV/AIDS crisis in Africa, what do you think we can achieve together that we'd never be able to achieve if we continued operating in our individual orbits?"

As people piped up with their fresh, solution-oriented ideas, energy and enthusiasm rose. As enthusiasm rose, our concentration became more focused, which caused a shared vision to emerge. Once we had a shared vision, we surrendered our egos in defense of it. And on and on it went. The point is, once we embraced *one* reality of leading from the fundamental state, *all* of the realities came into play.

Looking back, I'd say that by the end of the day, every one of us was a fundamental-state believer. We had experienced something transcendent in that meeting because each of us allowed the cause we were fighting for to eclipse personal wants, needs, and expectations. We'd all remember the event for a long, long time.

Select a Starting Point

During that meeting on HIV/AIDS, the starting point we selected to move us from the normal state to the fundamental state was this idea of keeping the vision clear. We'd all agreed to attend the forum because we believed that we could, in fact, achieve something together that we couldn't achieve alone. The opening question served to solidify that vision, and from there, the magnetic pull of the fundamental state was so strong that we couldn't help but walk right in.

Perhaps you face a current challenge that requires a little fundamental-state infusion. Which fully developed aspect of the fundamental state would help you the most right now? Choose one "starting point" from the list on the next page and circle it.

1. Possessing enthusiasm and energy

2. Concentrating on the needs of others

3. Leading with a surrendered ego

4. Leading from your passion

5. Keeping the vision clear

6. Taking risks

7. Making decisions . . . and making them confidently

8. Embracing change

What realities surrounding your current challenge prompted you to select the aspect you circled? Such as the reality of your present leadership stage, your present ministry season, a recent set of circumstances that has cropped up, or your wiring or temperament. (For example, when I was a leader in my twenties, I could have used a dose of "surrendered ego." When Willow undertook a large capital campaign recently, I needed an extra measure of risk-taking.) Write down your response below.

I believe that a huge part of a leader's role is declaring reality—both to himself and to those he leads and serves. Keep in mind the realities you just noted as you move to the next section.

Carve Out Sacred Spaces

Once you select a starting point for moving toward the fundamental state, it's necessary to carve out space to practice operating from it. Robert Quinn calls these occasions "sacred spaces."

Sacred spaces are momentary glimpses into the fundamental state that are carved out when trust-building exchanges occur. When you willingly carve out sacred spaces with those you lead or serve, you open yourself up to the idea that changing states of leadership really is possible. What's more, you model things like vulnerability, teachability, and a commitment to change for those around you.

During my meeting to find solutions for the HIV/AIDS crisis, our decision to enter the fundamental state didn't produce smooth sailing right away. As a group, we endured a few wobbly moments as we got our bearings in this new state of mind. But once someone extended an ounce of trust here by asking a thoughtful question, and an ounce of trust there by listening well, a sacred space was carved out. It was in that space that we collectively tested out our new fundamental-state posture.

If you wrestle with self-centeredness as a leader and choose to adopt an others-focused attitude as your starting point, I guarantee your new posture will take some getting used to. Things will feel awkward at first, but don't give up. Be intentional about setting aside time and energy to practice your new behavior so that you don't immediately revert back to the normal state.

Examples of Sacred Spaces

You carve out sacred spaces whenever you:

- Choose to be "known" by those you lead and serve.

- Truly engage with your team.

- Ask thoughtful questions to uncover problems or needs.

- Solicit opinions on issues affecting your team's ministry.

- Take time to check for understanding.

- Accept useful criticism.

- Explain the reasons why a decision is made or a direction is pursued.

- Set clear expectations, acknowledge people's efforts, and reward people's successes.

So where might you begin in practicing a new fundamental-state behavior?

- On the line below, write down your "fundamental state starting point"—the aspect of the fundamental state you circled on page 74.

- Locate that aspect on the chart below.

- Read through the questions noted to the right of it and answer each one honestly to yourself (you may be tempted to nuance your response, but I encourage you to declare the plain yes/no truth about each of your responses so that you can move forward with the task of making improvements).

QUESTIONS TO CATALYZE FUNDAMENTAL STATE BEHAVIOR

The Fundamental-State Aspect I'll Work on First

The Fundamental State	Questions to Ask of My Leadership
Possessing enthusiasm and energy	• Is my enthusiasm and energy for my role obvious to others? • Does the team I lead possess high enthusiasm and energy for the task at hand?
Concentrating on the needs of others	• Am I aware of the current resources my core team members need from me? • Do I seek to "learn from" instead of merely "get through" interactions with my team?
Leading with a surrendered ego	• Am I humble in interactions with my team? • Am I teachable in interactions with my team?
Leading from my passion	• Do I engage in the cause because of sheer passion? • Do I engage with my team because of sheer passion?
Keeping the vision clear	• Am I crystal clear about why I'm doing what I'm doing in my leadership role? • Do I clarify and promote the vision so often that my team knows I'm its strongest advocate?
Taking risks	• Am I known for taking risks? • Am I familiar enough with the nuances of the mission to know which risks to take in order to achieve it?
Making decisions confidently	• Do I make decisions when my team (or the cause) needs them to be made? • Do I stand beside my decisions once they're made, knowing I've chosen wisely?
Embracing change	• Am I willing to entertain discussions involving change that could advance the ministry cause? • Am I prone to approving beneficial changes?

Imagine for a moment that you said yes to both questions listed beside your fundamental state starting point, such as "Leading with a surrendered ego" or "Taking risks." Jot down a paragraph in the space below about how your leadership might change. How would you approach your ministry role? What would your communication patterns be? How would you deal with challenges or setbacks? What would you do when fears crept in?

How big is the gap between the vision you just wrote down and your current leadership reality?

The vision I wrote
down is a mirror
image of how I
operate today.

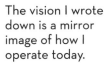 

The vision I wrote
down is the polar
opposite of my
current style.

What initial thoughts do you have about how you might tighten the gap? Capture your ideas in the space below.

The best leaders I know are able to detect the normal state as soon as even one of their toes has entered it. They have trained themselves to think like a fundamental-state leader so well that they automatically course-correct when human nature or circumstances threaten to catapult them into the normal state.

As you carve out sacred spaces to practice your fundamental-state behavior, you too will develop this auto-detection capability. Read on for one simple exercise that shows you how.

Pursue the Fundamental State

What follows is a straightforward way to head toward the fundamental state whenever you find yourself tangled up in normal-state mayhem. It involves three steps, and each one begins with the same letter, which I know pastor types especially will enjoy.

> Step 1: Rally an **ALLY.**
>
> Step 2: Invite **ACCOUNTABILITY.**
>
> Step 3: Take decisive and immediate **ACTION.**

Here's how these steps play out in everyday leadership. Let's say you're in a leadership team meeting and toward the end of the agenda you start bulldozing the rest of the group. You are wiped out from a grueling week, you're pressed for time because you're trying to actually make your son's soccer game for once, and you get the sense nobody in the room but you cares about a particular (highly important!) agenda item. Instead of concentrating on the needs of others, you force your opinions on everyone, paying no attention whatsoever to their (according to you) weak and ill-conceived input. *Somebody's* got to lead, right?

Things finally devolve to the point that even you become aware of your less-than-stellar behavior. You have a choice: you can stay in the normal state and self-destruct, or you can exhibit a dose of self-awareness and drop-kick yourself into the fundamental state.

1. To enter the fundamental state, declare an ALLY. Take a brief break, pull your team member Joe aside, and say, "Hey, Joe. I'm sinking here. I'm about to do an about-face and need your help. Just go with me, okay?"

   Resume the meeting and say, "Gang, I've been pretty self-focused for the last twenty minutes for a number of reasons, none of which excuses my behavior. Let's take a pass around the room so that I can hear your thoughts on the issue at hand. Joe, how about starting us off?"

2. Next, invite ACCOUNTABILITY. Once you're over the hurdle, push Pause on the meeting, tell your team you appreciate their reengagement, and shoot straight about your desire to concentrate on their needs and the needs of the shared mission you're all pursuing. Most importantly, when you interact with those team members later on, ask for their insights about whether your behavior really did improve and listen to their opinions with a cheerful heart (even if you think they're dead wrong!).

3. Finally, take decisive and immediate ACTION. Figure out the common themes you're hearing from team members you trust, and determine a plan for making necessary changes to your leadership style. My advice here is to strike while the iron is hot. If you're soliciting input on the same area of development eighteen months later, your team will sniff out something bogus in your desire to actually improve.

The framework is equally effective in one-on-one settings. If you can tell you're operating in a reactive or ego-driven mode, ask the other person to serve as an ally. Say, "I'd like to approach this subject in a proactive, others-focused way. Can you hold me accountable to that while I give you my thoughts on the matter?"

Page 81 includes a blank "Three-A" template for you to copy and use. Before moving ahead, designate a few meetings or interactions this week that can serve as practice ground for moving from the normal state to the fundamental state. You won't regret getting good at this transition, I assure you!

When you choose to enter the fundamental state with increasing frequency, the people around you will follow suit. As you carve out sacred spaces throughout the course of your everyday routine, you invite those you lead and serve to enter the fundamental state with you.

When you choose to enter the fundamental state with increasing frequency, the people around you will follow suit. As you carve out sacred spaces throughout the course of your everyday routine, you invite those you lead and serve to enter the fundamental state with you. And as was noted previously, it's here that holy discontent—yours *and* theirs—gets fed.

TRANSITIONING TO THE FUNDAMENTAL STATE

Select a meeting or interaction to use in evaluating whether or not you are exhibiting fundamental-state behavior. Following that encounter, use this form to jot down what unfolded and to track your progress. Make extra copies of this template as necessary.

Meeting or Interaction:

1 Rally an ALLY.

☐ Selected ahead of time

☐ Selected in the moment

Whom I chose and why:

2 Invite ACCOUNTABILITY.

What I said to let others know of my desire to improve and the feedback I received:

3 Take decisive and immediate ACTION.

What I am doing to self-correct:

4

CREATE A FEEDING FRENZY

I watched a show recently on the Discovery Channel about the behavior of red-bellied Brazilian piranhas (this is how exciting my life really is). What intrigued me was that, although it took the film crew a purported two weeks to capture the footage, once the fish were hungry enough and the conditions were right, the ensuing feeding frenzy was unstoppable. After the first piranha saw his dinner dart across the ocean floor, he was a goner. He eyed the goal, darted into action, and remained completely committed to the cause, which in this case was nabbing a fish. What's more, he seemed to move effortlessly, as if driven by some inner instinct that just demanded he achieve his objective. Fascinating!

Not surprisingly, thirty-five of his scaly pals were right on his tail, keeping perfect pace in hopes of tasting a little victory themselves.

As I watched this utterly captivating show, I was reminded of how cool it is that we leader types have the power to create similar feeding frenzies whenever we choose. When we decide to forsake the chaos and stress of ministry work and really home in on a goal, we have the unique ability to invite everyone we lead to follow us into battle. For this reason, the fundamental state is a terrible place to be if you're a loner. Once you enter, you'll find everyone else is compelled to join you there!

This makes sense, if you think about it: who *wouldn't* want to hang out with people who have abandoned their pride, their controlling behaviors, their irrational fears, and their need to please, and instead opted for passion-fueled, vision-centered, goal-oriented, risk-friendly living?

In your own sphere of influence—whether personal or professional—whom do you know who embodies these characteristics? How do you feel when you are in their presence? For example, think about how their fundamental-state behaviors impact you in the areas of respect, trust, confidence, and eagerness to follow their lead. Write down your thoughts below.

Here's the gut-level truth: as you choose to enter the fundamental state more and more, you will become this type of magnetizing person. What's more, organizationally speaking, you will cultivate an environment where things like trust, truth telling, and teamwork can move and live and breathe. And it's in this context that holy discontent gets nourished.

Since you're reading this guide, I presume that you're committed to learning how to live and lead from your holy discontent. But if you also desire to help those around you to do the same, you've got to take pains first to discover—and then help feed—the holy discontent of those you lead and serve. In chapter 3, you looked at the first of three choices leaders make to get this done, the choice to enter the fundamental state. Now let's look at choice number two, helping those you lead and serve to find their holy discontent.

CHOICE 2: HELP THOSE YOU LEAD AND SERVE FIND THEIR HOLY DISCONTENT

The first people to follow Jesus were career fishermen. In order to rally them around his cause, Jesus told them that if they went his way, they would be fishers of men. It was a mission that captivated their imaginations and elicited their best energies because they could relate so well to it. Their passion was fishing. By linking the overall vision to their individual passion, he provided the necessary on-ramp to ministry engagement.

Admittedly, you and I can't just "intuit" the same level of knowledge about those we lead. We have to apply a little elbow grease to get to the bottom of what makes them tick. Even so, it is quite possible to help others locate their areas of holy discontent.

Whenever leaders joyfully engage in the process of uncovering what is truest about those they lead and serve—their holy discontent—there is something a lot like Jesus going on in their minds and hearts.

As I have worked to help others discover their holy discontent, three guidelines always prove immensely helpful:

1. Hunt for insight.

2. Pay attention to themes.

3. Take a few test drives.

Let's take a closer look at each one.

> *Whenever leaders joyfully engage in the process of uncovering what is truest about those they lead and serve—their holy discontent—there is something a lot like Jesus going on in their minds and hearts.*

Hunt for Insight

It takes intentional effort to discover a person's holy discontent. Some people are reserved about sharing their passion pursuits; others simply don't know what they are passionate about. But if you are committed to helping them feed their holy discontent, you must first help them land on what it is.

Think of hunting for insight as an interpersonal treasure hunt. On a treasure hunt, you poise yourself to be awed by whatever interesting nuggets you find. As a leader, you can do the very same thing: prepare yourself to be awed, and then during interactions with colleagues, direct reports, or a supervisor, inject one or two substantive questions that touch the core of who they are and what makes them tick. I guarantee you'll pick up a few interpersonal nuggets.

A pastor I know was called to lead a church in the northwest. During his first few months, he kept an index card in his Bible for each of his three direct reports. Each card listed six or seven questions regarding their background, their motivations for ministry involvement, and their passions in life. As he gathered answers, he'd jot notes on the person's card. And whenever he happened to flip to that part of his Bible, he was reminded to pray for that person . . . as well as to gather answers to the remaining unanswered questions. The simple exercise helped him to build a bank of knowledge about the people he was responsible for—a bank he continues to make deposits in today.

Here are a few questions to ask of the people you lead and serve:

1. What motivates you?

2. What ignites passion in your heart?

3. Why did you first get involved in ministry?

4. What do you most enjoy about your ministry role?

5. What is your personal faith story? (What were you like before you met Christ, and what are you like now?)

6. What significant life events have shaped the way you approach your leadership position?

In the space below, write down what other questions you would imagine asking of those you lead and serve.

imagine

Only you know what type of forum would be conducive to exploring these questions with one or more people on your leadership team. Maybe it's a one-on-one lunch meeting. Or maybe it's a full leadership team meeting. It could be a day-long offsite meeting during which you could insert a holy-discontent segment onto the agenda. What type of forum would serve your team best? How might you pull it off?

Listen for Themes

After hunting for insights and then listening carefully, you may begin to notice that certain themes emerge in the answers you hear. Pay attention to themes! As you interact with those you serve and lead, listen for consistent conversational threads that reflect what they're most passionate about. If they simply can't engage in dialogue without mentioning their outrage over war, for instance, this ought to tell you something.

I know a worship pastor whose formal role revolves around singing but whose heart revolves around fighting for those who are oppressed and extremely impoverished. He can't *not* talk about these things!

A woman who is a key volunteer in her church's usher ministry can't open her mouth without mentioning God's love. She's a fanatic when it comes to evangelism!

A men's ministry director is committed to healthful living and is always giving unsolicited tips to men at his events: Drink more water! Ditch the sugar! Exercise once in a while!

Granted, your leaders' communication patterns may not be this obvious. The point is, as you interact with those you lead, make mental notes of topics that consistently crop up and take pains to explore what's behind them.

Based on your current knowledge of those you lead, what themes are you already aware of? Use the chart on page 89 to assess each member of your team.

WHAT MY TEAM MEMBERS ARE PASSIONATE ABOUT

Team Member	Conversational Themes (What He/She Always Seems to Talk About)

CREATEit

Communicating themes back to these people will undoubtedly help them to discover their holy discontent. Start now incorporating feedback phrases into your dialogue with the people you lead. Here are a few examples of what I'm talking about:

You seem to be energized by _____ .
What's behind your passion in this area?

Where did your interest in _____ come from?

When did your enthusiasm surrounding _____ start?

How did your concern for _____ surface?

● ●

What other questions might
you ask to help those you lead
uncover their holy discontent? question

Take a Test Drive

Once you have a sense for a person's holy discontent, pursue the task of organizing a few "holy discontent test drives."

I have a ministry colleague who is a highly energetic and compassionate individual. When Willow decided to shoot a video in central Africa to raise awareness about the HIV/AIDS pandemic, I brought her along on the trip. It was a test drive, of sorts—inviting someone to take a spin in an unusual situation, just to see if her holy discontent might show up. It did, and now she actively seeks out ways to support progress on a variety of fronts in Africa.

Take a few test drives with those you lead and serve. Invite them into challenging situations, offer them interesting resources, allow them to stretch their wings a little. Measure the risk and the reward of doing so, but always remember that by orchestrating a holy discontent test drive for someone you lead or serve, you might just catalyze the discovery of their holy discontent. More on this in the next section, "Choice 3."

Take this opportunity to capture any hunches you already have regarding test drives you could take with the key people you lead and serve. In the chart on the next page, note the ideas that come to mind when you think of unusual or challenging situations you could invite your team members into.

One Worship Pastor's Test Drive

A senior pastor I know sensed that Jon, his twenty-something worship leader, was struggling in his role. Jon was a fantastic soloist, a dynamic guitar player, and a well-loved member of the congregation. But he was also an introvert who often grew frustrated by how impersonal ministry sometimes felt in the large church he served.

My friend took a test drive with this young man by inviting him to begin mentoring up-and-coming musicians in groups of two or three. The camaraderie that developed was fueling to Jon, encouraging to the mentored musicians, and evident to the congregation, even from the stage. Jon's holy discontent, which dealt with small-group

continued on page 93

TEST DRIVES I CAN TAKE

Team Member	Test Drive Idea(s)

What fears or obstacles might stand in the way of pursuing the ideas you noted? Write down your thoughts in the space below.

CHAPTERfour

On the flip side, what do you stand to gain as it pertains to your team members' discovery of holy discontent by taking the risk to pursue one of your test-drive ideas?

Leaders who intentionally hunt for insights about those they lead and serve, pay attention to themes their team members convey, and then take the risk to orchestrate a few holy discontent test drives, are well positioned to begin the process of helping feed others' holy discontent.

discipleship, was born out of his own deep-seated needs regarding being known and being valued as an individual. Fortunately, my pastor friend was astute enough to pick up on this.

"My purpose wasn't to assemble a great team," he later admitted. "I just wanted to focus on leveraging people's passions and then let God draw the team together."

That's leadership wisdom at its finest.

CHOICE 3: PROVIDE WAYS TO FEED IT

As you seek to create a diligent or caring culture of leadership by helping others discover their holy discontent, it's critical that you work to provide opportunities to feed it. To get your arms around what this looks like (and what it *doesn't* look like), take a look at the following two stories, and answer the questions that follow.

Lead from the Fundamental State

THE STORY OF ADAM. The first story deals with a twenty-something pastor I'll call Adam and a boss who refused to lead from the fundamental state. Adam had recently graduated from seminary with honors and took a job with a local church as an associate pastor. Throughout his four-year seminary program, he was mentored by two of his favorite professors. As a result of sitting under the tutelage of such passionate instructors, something awakened in his heart. He realized that he could actually catalyze a passion for God's Word in other people the same way that these teachers had catalyzed it in him.

He decided that if he could give his life to *one* thing, it would be teaching seminary classes in a creative and compelling manner. Unfortunately, though, this wasn't what he thought he was training to do when he entered seminary. His plan all along was to rise through the church ranks to become a senior pastor—a plan his current senior pastor (and boss) was well aware of.

When Adam scheduled a meeting to tell this leader about his strong desire to teach, he received an unexpected response. "Trust me, Adam," the senior pastor said, "you do *not* want to teach! You are wired to be a senior pastor, you are perfectly suited to become a senior pastor, and that is exactly what you ought to do." End of discussion.

Adam walked out of that meeting deflated . . . but more resolute than ever about pursuing his passion for teaching.

THE STORY OF SUZANNE. The second story involves another pastor in her early twenties named Suzanne. Suzanne grew up in church and realized at a young age that she was gifted in graphic and creative arts. Rather than heading into a commercial job after graduating from seminary, she opted for a role leading the arts ministry at the church in her rural hometown.

She believed that the church should lead the charge in areas of design and relevant presentation of the church's mission to people living in surrounding neighborhoods. Although she didn't expect to radically change the world, she knew that her faithful contribution would allow at least one church to reflect God's creative excellence.

After two years in her role, Suzanne went to her senior pastor to ask for permission to build an official worship arts team, rather than continuing to do everything on her own. The pastor knew immediately that saying yes to the request would require people and equipment resources the church couldn't yet afford. However, instead of leading with this information, the senior pastor took a different approach. Knowing that God was up to something in Suzanne's heart, he posed questions like:

> Would you tell me more about your dream for a worship arts team?
>
> What prompted you to develop this idea?
>
> What is motivating you to pursue it?
>
> How can I serve your process of discovery until resources are available?

Suzanne emerged anything but deflated. Finally, someone understood her deepest passion pursuits and was ready to support them.

With both snapshots in mind—Adam and Suzanne—think about how you resonate with the leader in each story by answering the questions on the following page.

When have I behaved like Adam's pastor, operating from a place of presumption and expectation instead of mustering the energy and compassion to engage in the new reality of someone I lead?

What factors played into my behaving that way?

When have I behaved like Suzanne's pastor, operating from a place of openness and advocacy regarding the dreams of someone I lead?

What factors played into my behaving that way?

Did anyone provide creative outlets to feed *my* holy discontent along the way? Does my experience play into my willingness to help others feed their passion pursuits? If so, how?

Suzanne's pastor provided whatever resources he could until he was able to help her secure the funds for her larger dream. He established structured worship service planning meetings and invited her to lead them. He put her in touch with other arts leaders in their region who were willing to invest time and energy in her development. He even accompanied Suzanne and her husband to an arts conference in another state so she could get additional training and experience the best practices in her passion area.

Effective leaders *constantly* search out appropriate and creative outlets to help staff and key volunteers to feed their holy discontent. But to determine what is appropriate, leaders must first know how their people learn best.

Leverage Learning Style

I love to discover how people who work for me and with me learn and assimilate information. Years ago, I came across a great book on the subject by Marlene LeFever titled *Learning Styles.*[9] She describes four types of learners: imaginative, analytic, common sense, and dynamic. On the following page is a brief summary of each style.

FOUR LEARNING STYLES

Imaginative Learners

- Talk in broad overviews
- Learn by listening and sharing ideas
- Work best in a noisy and active setting
- Dislike long lectures and working alone
- Are idea people
- Are in tune with their feelings on a variety of subjects
- Learn by talking and enjoy role play
- Value people above products and see facts in relationship to people
- Love a colorful working situation
- Define themselves in terms of their friendships

Analytic Learners

- Like information presented logically and sequentially
- Value facts, figures, and the theoretical
- Value smart and wise people
- Set long-range plans and see their consequences
- Prefer a quiet learning situation
- Need competition
- Are impersonal
- Value being right
- Prefer to work alone
- Define themselves by how smart they are

Common-Sense Learners

- Move during the learning process
- Value "how-to" and lots of action
- Are goal-oriented
- See skills as knowledge
- Prefer to work alone and are impersonal
- Value strategic thinking
- Resent being given answers
- Excel in problem solving
- Dislike sitting quietly in learning setting
- Teach and learn through demonstration

Dynamic Learners

- Have experimental attitudes and behaviors
- Cultivate a well-developed sense of humor
- Demand flexibility and need options
- Are curious, insightful, and unpredictable
- Are future directed
- Want to do anything that breaks the mold
- Enjoy people and communicate with great skill
- Enjoy art forms that allow them to assert individuality
- Have strong intuition and make decisions based on hunches
- Work to make things better or different

CREATEit

Fill in the names of your key team members on the grid below; include yourself in a box, if you have a hunch regarding where you best fit.

MY TEAM'S LEARNING STYLES

Imaginative Learners	Analytic Learners

Common-Sense Learners	Dynamic Learners

(By the way, some people utilize two or even three learning styles. If you think someone might have more than one learning style, it's legal to place that person's name in more than one box.)

How do the characteristics in the list on page 99 manifest themselves in each person's behavior? What are the strengths you see in the way each person manifests this learning style? What about challenge areas? Capture your thoughts about three of the key people you lead in the space below.

1. Name: _____

    Strengths:

    Challenges:

2. Name: _____

    Strengths:

    Challenges:

3. Name: _____

    Strengths:

    Challenges:

The process of understanding how your team members learn is fluid. This is why it is critical that you engage in it *with your team members*, rather than presuming a style upon them. Talk to them about what you have observed about their learning style, and ask them what they see in their own life. Whatever you do, make the process fun and let it serve as an effective way to strengthen the relationships you have with the people God has placed around you in ministry. Then, as you search for ways to help feed their holy discontent, devise creative ways to leverage the learning style preferences that you've identified together.

For example, if you are leading an **imaginative learner**, you might help them feed their holy discontent by taking them out for coffee and talking about their passion pursuit instead of by sticking a book in their inbox. They'd probably be thrilled to attend a roundtable discussion with other imaginative learners on the topic of their holy discontent, whereas a one-directional lecture would bore them to tears.

Analytic learners might respond well to a scheduled conference call with an expert in their passion area or may enjoy receiving the latest report from a well-known research group that validates or challenges some aspect of their holy discontent.

Common-sense learners would likely jump at the chance to conduct a research project dealing with their holy discontent and report back their findings. Or just think of how inspiring an on-the-job site visit with someone who works in their area of holy discontent would be for them!

You might consider asking a **dynamic learner** to lead a brainstorming session about what a ministry focused on their holy discontent could become and what resources it would take to see it come to fruition. Or devise some other plan that leverages their insatiable appetite for envisioning and then ushering in the future state of whatever they're passionate about.

Keeping your top three people in mind, use the chart on page 103 to note a few appropriate ideas for engaging them in the process of feeding their holy discontent.

STYLE-APPROPRIATE IDEAS FOR
FEEDING MY TEAM'S HOLY DISCONTENT

Team Member	Style-Appropriate Ideas for Feeding Holy Discontent

I hope you'll choose to be the one to release those you lead to their God-given holy discontent. You never know what young Martin Luther King Jr. or Mother Teresa or Bono you might be leading. Take a pass, and everyone loses: you, those you lead, and the entire sphere of potential influence those individuals represent. But get it right, and potentially, the whole *world* gets changed.

Trust the Process

Admittedly, helping others to find and feed their holy discontent can be a messy and unpredictable process. It's certainly more art than science. But whenever I talk to leaders who are struggling to help their team members in this regard, I always encourage them simply to trust the process of living and leading from holy discontent.

The process, illustrated on the chart below, includes the general progression you have worked through to this point: find your own holy discontent; feed it once you find it; use your topped-off energy supply to enter the fundamental state as frequently as possible; and intentionally invite others into the process.

THE PROCESS OF LIVING AND LEADING FROM HOLY DISCONTENT

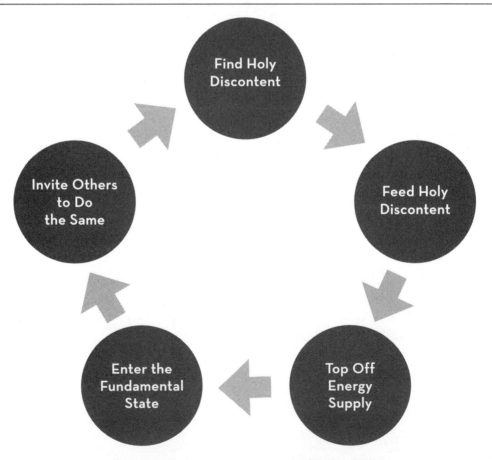

A ministry leader in the South is working through this progression about as effectively as anyone I know. When asked about her holy discontent, Shannon Ford can point to evidence as far back as her elementary school days. As a third grader, she defended helpless kids who were being bullied by the cool crowd. In junior high, she went on a local mission trip and was exposed to the harsh realities of poverty, injustice, and oppression.

Although she didn't know she was dealing with a fully fledged holy discontent, she naturally gravitated toward "feeding" opportunities throughout high school, college, and her early career. She went on mission trips, lived overseas for various stints to experience lifestyles different from her own privileged upbringing, attended classes that exposed her to the troubling realities faced by more than two-thirds of the world, and read everything she could get her hands on so she'd know where to focus her efforts. Wherever she saw injustice prevail, Ford wanted to root it out.

Her burning bush conversation with God occurred on an otherwise average day, when she sensed God saying to her, "What else do you need from me to go?"

She knew the "go" referred to an opportunity she had to join a church staff in Houston, Texas, that served an urban community of adults in recovery. At the time, she was working in downtown Chicago for an award-winning and innovative nonprofit that helped people with various addictions and mental illness create productive, fulfilling lives. Somehow, she'd never envisioned herself heading up the counseling department for a denominational agency. But still, she went.

The majority of people in the congregation Ford serves have suffered an addiction to something, be it drugs, alcohol, sex, gambling, or a whole host of other issues. The path back to a functional life isn't always easy and is often laden with injustices of another kind. It's messy and imperfect, she admits, but the proximity to real-life struggles keeps her grounded in her faith, keeps her holy discontent fed, and as a result, keeps her fuel level extremely high for doing the hard work of ministry.

Ford wasn't given a staff team when she arrived, so she went out and rallied a dozen volunteers to help her achieve her vision of holistic ministry—treating people's physical, psychological, emotional, and practical life-skills needs, in addition to their spiritual ones.

She approached treatment and community development centers whose mission statements talked about serving "the least of these" and invited them into partnership. Once on board, she fanned their flames of holy discontent for righting societal wrongs by establishing programs that help strengthen frail people, teach uneducated people, free addicted people, resource poor people, and instill hope in those whose hope was long gone.

For Ford, living and leading from her holy discontent—and teaching others to do the same—didn't eradicate the tough stuff of ministry. In addition to the typical burdens of administrative work, counseling needs, and too many demands on each day's time, she also faces personal challenges. She is often misunderstood by family members and judged even by her closest friends for embracing people who are so broken and so different.

But as to whether or not it's worth it, she quotes Jesus' exhortation to "heal the sick, raise the dead, cleanse those who have leprosy, drive out demons. Freely you have received, freely give."[10] With a grin, she then adds, "A little speed bump every now and then? Bring it on! I wouldn't live life any other way."

Think for a moment about Ford's comment that she "wouldn't live life any other way." In the space below, note what percentage of the people you lead or serve would say they are so satisfied and feel so valued in their ministry role that they too wouldn't live life any other way.

note

How might your leadership look different if you fostered an environment where 100 percent of your team agreed with the statement, "I wouldn't live life any other way"?

An amazing thing happens when you lead with an attitude that says to those around you, "I know you; I care about you; now, how can I help?" To get there, though, requires that you actually know your people and have enough of a fuel supply to care genuinely for their needs.

As you get serious about engaging in this manner with each person you lead, I think you'll find that the sheer momentum catapults you into an entirely new stratum of leadership effectiveness.

Part III

INSTIGATE

Connecting the Dots of Holy Discontent

5

FIND COLLECTIVE HOLY DISCONTENT IN YOUR STAFF

Nearly all of our efforts as leaders are applied for the goal of *initiating movement*. Specifically, under the Holy Spirit's guidance, we try to bring about movement in individuals' spiritual journeys that includes softening their hearts, opening their eyes, reordering their priorities, and refreshing their hope.

We labor to see seekers move toward believing, believers move toward maturity, isolationists move toward community, gifted ones move toward serving, and donors move toward giving. And when movement happens on any of these fronts, we feel the unmistakable buzz of knowing we were used by God to do something we couldn't orchestrate on our own.

I happen to think, however, that a very special buzz is reserved for those occasions when such movement occurs across an entire team, or even an entire church. This is, after all, the primary reason leaders must learn to live and lead from their holy discontent: not so that they can take their newfound limitless energy supply and head to the golf course, but so they can approach God's calling with fresh wind in their sails every single day they take to the waters of ministry.

In parts I and II of this companion guide, you explored how to find and feed your own holy discontent, as well as how to help find and feed the holy discontent of those you lead and serve. In this part, you will explore the communal implications of holy discontent. In order to connect the dots of holy discontent in your leadership environment, it's important to address this question: *What happens when God-breathed movement in the life of an individual morphs into collective holy discontent?*

GOD-ORDAINED MOVEMENTS

The greatest movements in history occurred because individuals were willing to devote themselve fully to the cause of Christ. Their burning-bush moments left them so revved up that they simply couldn't imagine giving their lives to lesser dreams.

The greatest movements in history occurred because individuals were willing to devote themselves *fully* to the cause of Christ. Their burning-bush moments left them so revved up that they simply couldn't imagine giving their lives to lesser dreams. It was true for Mother Teresa. It was true for Martin Luther King Jr. It was true for Billy Graham. And it's true for you and me, assuming God does something fantastic in and through our lives!

Do you agree or disagree with the statement, *The greatest movements in history occurred because individuals were willing to devote themselves fully to the cause of Christ?* What might it reveal about God's character that he tends to catalyze movement in the hearts of individuals before he draws additional adherents to the cause?

Regardless of whether you lead an entire church, a ministry team, a group of three teenagers with big dreams, or some other collection of people, your role is to keep one eye on the horizon and stay ready to spot God-ordained movements, seize them, and celebrate them once they have occurred. Sometimes the movement begins in your heart. Other times, in the heart of someone you lead or serve. Either way, the goal of the three chapters in Part III is to whet your appetite for joining God in the kingdom-building endeavors he has reserved for *your* team, wherever and however they might appear.

Leaning into collective holy discontent follows a similar progression as that of leaning into personal holy discontent:

- **Find it** in your staff.

- **Feed it** with your systems.

But there is more. Because once you find it and feed it, you must not quit until you:

- **Ennoble it** through your strategy.

In this chapter, you will explore the first part of the progression, where to *find* holy-discontent-inspired movements of God.

Finding Collective Holy Discontent

As I visit churches all over the world, I'm struck that the ones that seem to make the most progress are those whose ministry teams are rallied around holy discontent. Someone in their midst had a burning passion to right a wrong in this world, and now, as a result, the entire group is taking serious kingdom ground.

To find the *collective* holy discontent of those you lead, take a good, hard look at the staff members God has placed around you. They are not there by accident! God has a specific plan in store for you and those you lead and serve, collectively. Gather information about their past experiences as a team, their present joys and annoyances, and their future dreams. Your diligent efforts in these three areas will likely yield insights regarding what God is up to in your midst.

Note: In several of the activities to follow, you will be asked to evaluate "your team." If you are the senior leader in your church, then technically *every* staff person is part of your team. I encourage you to start by evaluating a smaller segment of your leadership team, like your board of directors, your elder board, or your senior leadership team. Same goes for leaders of large, individual ministries such as students or small groups: select your direct reports or a key volunteer team instead of trying to include scores of people in your assessment.

WHERE HAVE THEY BEEN?

As you seek out holy-discontent-inspired movement in your team, first take a look back at your team's shared history. Consider these three leaders' situations:

- A student ministry leader's team—comprised of a handful of staff members and hundreds of volunteers—lost a freshman girl to suicide. She took her own life after discovering she was pregnant. The experience caused this team to devote themselves to teaching kids about issues such as purpose, intimacy, and forgiveness with greater fervor and greater intentionality.

- Nearly half of a senior pastor's leadership team had suffered personal financial ruin at some point in their lives because of poor decisions. Now when it comes time to tend to their church's annual budgeting process, they dive in with reckless abandon and sharp pencils. They refuse to let their congregation suffer the same ill effects of financial neglect they faced.

- A worship arts director's all-volunteer team shares the experience of having been told as school-aged kids that they'd never make it as artists. Now they rally around the belief that *everyone* is an artist, created in the image of the Creator, and seek to call out oft-suppressed artistic contributions from each person in the congregation.

The common denominator in each of these stories is that the team's passion pursuits could be traced back to shared history.

Every team has a story, including your team. Whether you lead paid staff or volunteers, the first place to look for collective holy discontent is in your team's shared history. Start by capturing your own snapshot of your team's history and culture. Read the instructions on the following page; then use the chart on page 116 titled "Our Collective History: My Perspective" to respond.

1. What are the major, significant events—or defining moments—in your team's history? Consider both the positive and negative experiences that have shaped your team. Write them in the center column of the chart.

2. When did these events take place? Note the timeframe of each event in the left column.

3. What was the overall effect on the team? Indicate your response in the right column using one of the following four marks:

  ++ extremely positive

  + positive

  – negative

  – – extremely negative

Pay Attention to Your Collective History

As you revisit your team's collective history, consider how the past has shaped their present approach to ministry. Specifically, focus on the shared aspects of their:

- **Motivations for ministry involvement**—reasons for being roused to action toward desired spiritual goals or outcomes

- **Attitudes toward ministry**—beliefs, values, and dispositions affecting how roles get played out

- **Spiritual disciplines**—practices that improve strength or self-control

- **Work habits**—patterns of behavior that accompany productivity

- **Preferences and idiosyncrasies**—attributes that are distinctive or peculiar to a particular team

- **Responses to conflict**—the manner in which interpersonal challenges are managed and overcome

OUR COLLECTIVE HISTORY: MY PERSPECTIVE

	Timeframe	Significant Event	Impact (++/+/–/– –)
Ex.	January '95	New leadership team installed as result of church staff reorganization	–

revisit

What did it feel like to revisit the journey you and your team have been on? What did you learn about yourself, and what did you learn about your team, as you noted the significant events you have shared?

Now make looking back on your shared history a collective effort. Meet with your team to get their take on how the team came to exist and the defining moments that most significantly impacted it. Use the chart on page 118 "Our Collective History: My Team's Perspective" to capture the defining moments they share.

OUR COLLECTIVE HISTORY: MY TEAM'S PERSPECTIVE

Timeframe	Significant Event	Impact (++/+/–/– –)

After you capture your team's perspective on their shared history, consider the following two questions.

1. How did your team respond to the history-gathering process you engaged them in? Check all that apply.

    My team was:

    ❏ Shocked that I took time to do this exercise with them

    ❏ Unfazed; they are accustomed to the process of staying in touch with our team's history

    ❏ Surprised to learn things about themselves or the team they didn't know

    ❏ Reminded of how much the team has been through together

    ❏ Honored to have me take a genuine interest in their collective history

    ❏ Energized by the positive memories

    ❏ Aware of God's faithfulness throughout the team's journey

    ❏ Full of anticipation about what God has in store next

    ❏ Other: _____

2. What fresh revelations did the team make about their shared history as you probed the past with them? For example, was there general consensus or disagreement regarding the events that shaped them? What themes emerged? What emotions were stirred up?

Based on your own reflections and those of your team, what are the three most significant "defining moments" that have shaped the culture of your team?

Defining Moment 1:

Defining Moment 2:

Defining Moment 3:

Looking at your list, can you identify one common denominator that is shared by the three defining moments? For example, perhaps all of your team's primary defining moments reflect perseverance or abundance or immense blessing. Maybe the common denominator is an inhumane work pace or, on the other end of the spectrum, healthy, measured living. Maybe it's consistent change. If you had to boil it down to *one thing*, what is the sole common denominator for your team? Write down your thoughts in the space below.

Searching out a team's history can yield profound insights about what God may be stirring up in your collective soul. Consider what you gleaned from your team's shared past that might explain the "why" behind their current, collective posture in the following six key areas:

1. Motivations for ministry involvement

2. Attitudes toward ministry

3. Spiritual disciplines

4. Work habits

5. Preferences and idiosyncrasies

6. Responses to conflict and fear

1. **MOTIVATIONS FOR MINISTRY INVOLVEMENT:** Does the team contribute out of compulsion or out of passion? Why?

2. **ATTITUDES TOWARD MINISTRY:** Do team members collectively tend toward proactivity or procrastination? Do they tend to be trusting or suspicious of people? Do they respect organizational structure or do as they please and ask forgiveness later? Are they laid-back or high-strung, optimistic or pessimistic, abundance oriented or scarcity oriented, cheerful or dismal, gregarious or reserved? Why?

3. **SPIRITUAL DISCIPLINES:** Does the team pray together? Fast together? Challenge one another? Hold one another accountable? Encourage one another? Love one another? Why or why not?

4. **WORK HABITS:** Does the team have a strong or weak work ethic? Do they rise to the occasion or flail about when the going gets tough? Do they support or push back against leadership decisions? Why?

5. **PREFERENCES AND IDIOSYNCRASIES:** Is the team generally high- or low-maintenance? Do small annoyances create chaos, or does it take a lot to aggravate the team? Why?

6. **RESPONSES TO CONFLICT AND FEAR:** Does the team handle conflict and conflict resolution well? Do they avoid difficult conversations and people, or are they proactive in seeking solutions and reconciliation? Why?

Before moving to the next section, jot down in the space below any additional thoughts you have regarding how your team's shared history may be influencing their present behavior.

WHERE ARE THEY NOW?

Now that you've recollected your team's milestones, as well as made some observations about how those events influence their present behavior, consider what aspects of your team's current involvements elicit the greatest amount of passion from them.

Joys

As you consider their current workload, what projects, challenges, or interactions seem to fire them up the most?

Annoyances

What things annoy them most? What types of projects, challenges, or interactions collectively *can't they stand* (in the "holy discontent" use of the phrase)?

Where do you see evidence of God's movement within your team, based on the joys and annoyances you noted? For example, does it seem God is providing opportunities that leverage the team's particular areas of joyfulness? Or is he building up their character or patience by challenging them to overcome or help solve their areas of annoyance?

When you commit yourself to finding holy-discontent-inspired movement within the members of your team, you begin to see reality from God's perspective instead of your own. You develop thicker skin for hearing their frustrations, greater tolerance for bearing their burdens, and a keener eye for seeing their potential . . . which brings us to the third consideration for finding collective holy discontent, "Which way are they headed?"

> "When you commit yourself to finding holy-discontent-inspired movement within the members of your team, you begin to see reality from God's perspective instead of your own."

WHICH WAY ARE THEY HEADED?

The dreams of your team represent the hope of your ministry's future. Specifically, those things they're utterly devoted to—as well as the things they just can't stand—very possibly represent what God hopes to accomplish on a *grander* scale right there in your midst.

Your Current Team

A student ministry leadership team recently rolled out their "More than Four" vision. Credible surveys showed that if current trends held, only 4 percent of their twenty-something generation would surrender their hearts to Christ during the course of their lifetime. It was a reality this youth group refused to accept. They prayed for direction, rallied their resources, and set out to change reality.

The vision they now talk about, preach about, pray about, think about, and live out daily in practical ways says, in effect, "We will not rest until we reach more than 4 percent of our generation for Christ."

• •

In the space below, note the collective ministry-related dreams you feel your team may be dreaming.

dream

When we pursue our God-given holy-discontent-inspired dreams for righting wrongs, we become "an unstoppable force for good in the world."[11] What would look different in the lives of the people you seek to serve if your team achieved their dream? (For example, when the student ministry team achieves their goal, thousands of young people will have surrendered their lives to Christ. As a result, those new believers' habits and priorities will reflect God's wisdom instead of their own, and for the first time in their lives, their future hope will burn brightly.) Write your thoughts below.

In what ways does your team reflect the godly characteristics they're hoping to bring about in other people's lives? (For example, the student ministry team might note the ways they currently reflect fully surrendered lives and habits/priorities that manifest God's wisdom rather than their own.) Capture your thoughts below.

On the flip side, where do you see gaps between the team's present behaviors or attitudes and the vision they hope to realize? (For example, the student ministry team discovered that, while they advocated leaning into God's wisdom to those they tried to reach, they themselves were relying on their own strength to bring about change in their generation. They devoted themselves to hour-long sunrise prayer meetings for sixty days in order to reestablish their reliance on God's resources to accomplish the vision he'd given them.) Where do you see gaps? Record them below.

Staying in touch with your team's dreams will provide you loads of input to know how to help feed their holy discontent, which will be addressed in chapter 6.

Team Members to Come

Allow me a brief tangent here regarding how holy discontent can aid the hiring process as you add new team members to your team.

In *Holy Discontent* you were introduced to Eleanor Josaitis, cofounder of Focus: HOPE, the Detroit-based civil and human-rights group. A primary reason the organization has sustained its original passion over the decades is because Eleanor *hires to holy discontent*.

Every Focus: HOPE job candidate meets one-on-one with Eleanor prior to being hired. During that meeting, Eleanor reviews significant events in the organization's history, explaining how Focus: HOPE was founded, how the mission was established, and how they remain firmly committed to the same cause even today. As she concludes her presentation, she then asks the potential colleague if they can support the mission and serve as an ambassador for Focus: HOPE.

She delivers her presentation with passion and power—emotions prospective employees can't help but pick up on—and then draws out of them any personal experiences that may feed into their passion for fighting racism and poverty. According to Eleanor, it's easy to detect whether the applicant is willing and/or able to match her enthusiasm for the cause.

> "Colleagues are truly unified in their commitment to Focus: HOPE's mission. From their very first day, it is clear what they are working toward, which provides them a framework for assessing everything they do. What's more, they know that every single person they work with is committed to the same goal."

The result is that colleagues who make the cut are truly unified in their commitment to the mission. From their very first day, it is clear what they are working toward, which provides them a framework for assessing everything they do. What's more, they know that every single person they work with is committed to the same goal.

To this point in time, what factors have played the biggest role in determining who you add to your team? Check all that apply.

- ❏ Competency/skill mix
- ❏ Spiritual gift mix
- ❏ Ministry experience
- ❏ Professional/corporate experience
- ❏ Personality/temperament
- ❏ Professional appearance/presence
- ❏ References
- ❏ Test scores (aptitude, leadership style, etc.)
- ❏ Your own "gut" or instincts about the person

How might your hiring process look different if an emphasis on a person's holy discontent were added to this mix?

What risks would you face by emphasizing a person's holy discontent—their primary passion areas and their ability/willingness to support the passions of your existing team—as your hiring criteria?

I encourage you to look through the lens of holy discontent the next time you face a hiring decision. Passion begets passion, and when you are committed to adding "like-passioned" people to your team, you give God a green light to continue the work he hopes to accomplish in your midst.

6

FEED COLLECTIVE HOLY DISCONTENT WITH YOUR SYSTEMS

As you might expect, once you help your team find their collective holy discontent, the next step is to provide appropriate ways to feed it. The most effective tool in a leader's arsenal in this regard is the organizational system, which is simply a structured approach to accomplishing an overall goal.

Organizational systems serve as the connective tissue that holds ministry life together. They have inputs, they have processes, and they have outcomes. Some are crafted with incredible care and intention, while others evolve rather accidentally. Either way, organizational systems may be useful mechanisms for beckoning God's movement within your team.

We'll evaluate three systems in light of holy discontent—communications, finances, and rewards. Let these examples serve as models for how to scrutinize the other systems you maintain, such as your hiring, orientation, or training systems, or your systems for creating bylaws, volunteerism policies, performance appraisals, or membership parameters.

FEEDING HOLY DISCONTENT WITH COMMUNICATIONS

You feed collective holy discontent with your communications system when you infuse mutual information exchanges with language that reflects what people are most passionate about. In other words, when you link why you do what you do in ministry as a *team* with why you do what you do as *individuals*, holy discontent smiles.

I always enjoy hearing how various ministries at Willow vie for their particular approach to accomplishing our vision. If you listen to the small group folks, you'll come away thinking Willow's vision hinges on establishing more groups. Bigger groups. *Deeper* groups. If you listen to the evangelists, you'll hear them blow off the groupies and say the *real* bang for our buck lies in attracting more seekers and persuading them to go God's way with their lives. Women's ministry says they need more women; men's needs more men; children's thinks everything revolves around kids, and on and on it goes.

If you don't have a proper perspective on this dynamic, it can turn you gray in a heartbeat! But here is what I'm learning as it pertains to holy discontent: rather than wishing everyone in every ministry would just get on the same page, my job is to find ways to leverage passion by *really listening* to what each group is saying about why they do what they do, both among themselves and beyond themselves to the people they seek to serve.

Internal Messaging

Internal messaging is what you tell yourself about why you do what you do; it reflects the underlying motivation that drives your ministry involvement. Consider your own team. What do they say in the safety of their group about why they do what they do? What do they talk about with each other and with you in the hallways, during staff meetings, after ministry events? Fill in the dialog bubbles on page 133 with the kinds of things you hear your team members saying these days.

MY TEAM'S INTERNAL MESSAGES

Not long ago I realized that so much of my ministry life had been spent persuading people to think a certain way or do a certain thing that I had forgotten how to listen well. I persuaded elders to release funds, I persuaded staff members to get on board with a vision, I persuaded Willow's participating members to suit up and get in the serving game, and I persuaded seekers to give God a chance. If someone didn't conform to my way of thinking or to my action plan, I figured I hadn't persuaded them adequately enough, and so I'd up my persuasion tactics a little more.

Once I saw the negative effect this was having on my leadership effectiveness, I adopted a new approach. When one of my team members dissented on a particular subject, instead of jumping into persuasion mode, I took a deep breath and then took time to ask a few follow-up questions, such as these:

- You may have a point there. What's driving your opinions about this issue?

- Can you help me get my arms around your perspective on this?

- You seem to feel differently than when we last spoke. What do you think is influencing your shift in direction on this subject?

- I'm interested in how you arrived at your conclusion. Would you mind walking me through the train of thought that brought you here?

Perhaps you can relate to the dynamic I describe. What aspects of your leadership style may be inhibiting your ability to really hear what your team is saying about why they do what they do? Note your thoughts on the chart below, as well as what you might do to overcome each inhibitor. I've included my example to get you started.

	What's Inhibiting My Ability to Absorb My Team's Internal Messages?	Approach I Could Take to Overcome this Inhibitor
Ex.	My proneness to persuade instead of really probe others' opinions	Slow down; take time to ask clarifying questions of my team

Consider conveying the messages you hear back to your team. Ask them to assess whether these are the messages they intend to convey. Then challenge them to pinpoint what God may be saying to them collectively as a result.

External Messaging

There's another type of messaging that often reveals what God is up to in a given group: *external messaging*, or what you tell others about why you do what you do.

A church in the Midwest attributes more than 80 percent of its recent growth to an influx of Vietnamese refugees to their nearby neighborhoods. You can't walk through their church offices without being bombarded by their three-word holy discontent: "Free to Serve." Free to Serve posters line every wall, including the ones in the bathroom. They refuse to remain enslaved to the things that once held them captive. Instead, they let the political tyranny they faced fire them up to help other people find freedom from all sorts of oppression.

This is a perfect example of how external messaging can feed holy discontent, and the best leaders I know lean into this aspect of their communications system with great intention and frequency. They figure out what language draws out their people's deepest passions, and then they say it again and again, until the message becomes part of the team's vernacular.

If I dropped in unannounced for a visit with your team, what primary external message might be plastered on the walls? Fill in the one-line message that reflects why your team does what they do on the poster to the right.

Your communication system is an extraordinarily powerful tool for drawing out and helping feed your team's collective holy discontent. Leader, pay close attention to the internal and external messages you hear! God might just be at work.

FEEDING HOLY DISCONTENT WITH FINANCES

In addition to managing your communication system, the choices you make regarding management of team finances have dramatic implications on how effectively you feed collective holy discontent.

What Gets Measured?

I know of a church that is so committed to introducing underresourced people to the gospel that they actually *pay* men and women who are homeless three dollars every time they attend a weekend worship service. I imagine more than a few sparks flew during the board meeting to push that decision through. But once the plan was in place, just think how much collective holy discontent got fed each week! When they set out to determine ministry effectiveness each month, one measurement they consistently take is how many three-dollar coupons were redeemed.

Complete the chart below by noting what your team measures to determine ministry effectiveness, as well as the reason(s) why for each item.

WHAT OUR TEAM MEASURES AND WHY

What Gets Measured (How We Know We're "Succeeding")	Why We Measure It

Is there a general sense that the items you noted on the chart above link directly to your team's current passions or future dreams? What might change in your measurement system if you were to more closely align the things you measure with the things your team is most passionate about? Write your thoughts below.

What Gets Resourced?

From a fiscal perspective, it's important to pay attention not only to what your team measures, but also to what is being resourced.

In *Holy Discontent* you read of Nehemiah's trek to rebuild the wall of Jerusalem. Every time I come across the story, I'm struck by one question: *What if the king had denied Nehemiah the necessary resources for completing the task God had called him to complete?*

When Nehemiah approached the king to tell of his burden for rebuilding the wall surrounding Jerusalem, King Artaxerxes gave his cupbearer preferential status, a traveling companion, and assurance of safe passage from Persia to Nehemiah's ancestral home. Not to mention permission to be away from his post for more than a decade.

Imagine you're Artaxerxes in that situation. How do you determine whether resourcing Nehemiah's request will aid God's agenda or not? How do you know if it's a risk you should take?

· ·

Now think about the current "asks" your team is making of you. How do you determine which ones to resource and which to deny?

With King Artaxerxes' example fresh on your mind, I wonder, are you risking enough to feed your team's passion pursuits? Think of the last few times you denied your team a resource they requested, whether it was permission to attend a conference, the addition of a new teammate, a tool to enable work productivity, or something else they thought might aid their effective ministry. On the chart below, note the request that was made and the reason for declining it.

RECENT RESOURCE REQUESTS

Resource Requested	Reason for My "No"

How might your responses have been different if you had factored *holy discontent* into the decision?

FEEDING HOLY DISCONTENT
WITH REWARDS

A third system to leverage in feeding collective holy discontent is your rewards system. I think of ministry-team rewards as falling into two basic categories: formal and informal.

Formal Rewards

Formal rewards are all the structured, predictable ways you affirm your team's continued effort to push the ministry-vision ball up the field. If crafted carefully, in addition to honoring your team, these rewards can actually feed collective holy discontent.

I know of a ministry leader who honors one volunteer each month for outstanding service. Instead of receiving gift cards or movie tickets, though, the winner is invited to a "Passion Brunch," where he or she is given a thirty-minute time slot on the agenda to educate the ministry's staff team about their most passionate area of ministry interest. Over the years, every imaginable topic has been covered, from the benefits of homeschooling, to the spread of the gospel in Indonesia, to keeping kids drug-free, to learning how to read a profit-and-loss statement. The event is always full of interesting facts, lots of laughs, and fascinating windows into people's passion pursuits.

On the chart on page 141, "Modify Formal Rewards to Feed Holy Discontent," note three of the formal rewards you use to affirm your team's efforts on an ongoing basis. Think about the people these rewards are intended to serve. Factor in how the reward evolved, as well as how well-suited it is for feeding holy discontent. Use the chart to evaluate three such rewards. Then use this template as a model for how you assess the effectiveness of *all* of your team's formal rewards.

MODIFY FORMAL REWARDS TO FEED HOLY DISCONTENT

	Formal Reward	Group It Intends to Serve	How the Reward Evolved	How It Feeds Holy Discontent
Ex.	"Passion Brunch"	Each month's "most valuable" volunteer	After the new vision was rolled out, each ministry was challenged to think creatively about how to show-case people who were living out the values we said we esteemed in our overall ministry	Gives each honoree a platform for sharing holy discontent and how that passion pursuit links to his or her ministry role

Informal Rewards

Informal rewards are less-structured ways to acknowledge a team's exceptional efforts. I recently conducted a videotaped interview with a professional screenwriter and producer. The interview required several months of preparation leading up to three very long days on the shoot. When all was said and done, I decided the best way I could reward the seven crew members who had worked so hard was to get together for pizza and a movie—one written by the guy we'd just interviewed.

My approach might seem cheap, but trust me, when people whose primary passions involve producing, directing, lighting, staging, and editing video that will hopefully change lives hang out for a few hours watching a well-crafted movie, their weariness gets replaced by fresh energy for their roles. This is the power of leaning into collective holy discontent!

On page 62 in chapter 3, you noted a major "hill" or initiative you and your team currently face. What holy-discontent-infused informal rewards might you insert along the way to keep your team inspired to complete the overall mission? Brainstorm your ideas using the following four questions as a guide.

1. **What competencies and personal character qualities will be required of your team in order to accomplish the mission?**
   For example, in the video interview example I noted above, the "hill" the crew faced—producing a stellar product—required things such as technical expertise, solid project management skills, and personal management so they'd stay healthy, rested, and emotionally strong heading into a taxing shoot.

2. **How long will it take to accomplish the mission?** For example, the shoot required three months of preparation, three days to execute, and five weeks to edit and finalize post-production work.

3. **When is the next natural place on the project plan to stop and acknowledge the team's progress?** For example, I knew going into the project that based on my travel schedule, as well as the crew's other projects, there would be four critical junctures where I could thank the team for their work firsthand: at project inception, just before the shoot, immediately following the shoot, and right after the screening of the finished product.

4. **What are your holy-discontent-feeding ideas for how you might reward their efforts at those critical junctures?** For example, the pizza-and-a-movie reward I offered my crew. Fill in as many ideas as you can think of.

a.

b.

c.

d.

e.

I hope you'll commit yourself to getting good at leveraging your formal *and* informal rewards system. You have incredible power to feed your team's passions while simultaneously calling them to care about the things that will help God accomplish his purposes.

> "You have incredible power to help feed your team's passions while simultaneously calling them to care about the things in this world that need to be set right."

I watch pastors and leaders use this power wisely all the time by finding innovative ways to expose their team to everything from the plight of the poor to the mayhem that ensues from a poorly planned youth retreat. Stay close to the passions of those you lead and serve. Ask God for direction. And then reward your team for a job well done! Just be sure to feed a little holy discontent while you're at it.

7

ENNOBLE COLLECTIVE HOLY DISCONTENT THROUGH YOUR STRATEGY

Most every church I come across seeks to win people to Christ and then grow them into fully devoted followers of Christ. But the way this gets worked out—the *how* of that vision—is often what distinguishes one church from another. God's ideal plan for how your ministry vision gets executed might just be connected to the collective holy discontent of the people in your midst.

You have spent the bulk of the last two chapters exploring ways to find and then feed God-ordained movements that lean into collective holy discontent. Now you will explore what to do when one of these movements shows up by answering the following two questions:

- How will you recognize movements of God?

- How much should God's movement impact your vision?

HOW WILL YOU RECOGNIZE MOVEMENTS OF GOD?

Rarely does a leader ever set out to *create* a movement. In other words, movements are typically called movements only in hindsight. This is especially true as it pertains to ministry leadership, where our entire world revolves around God's mysterious, unknowable ways—a dynamic that can make it tough to spot a movement when it's on the horizon.

The best advice I can give you as you seek to see God move is to trust the Holy Spirit who lives inside of you to reveal to you what you need to know, when you need to know it. I'm sure people would be surprised to know just how much of my leadership involves my responding to "promptings" instead of relying on logical arguments or formulaic approaches. For me, the most effective way to be ready to steward movements of God is to have a vibrant, active prayer life. In the next section, you will be led through a process of praying for your team. You may wish to write out your prayers or simply pray them. Do whatever feels most comfortable for you.

So, then, what might you pray for? For starters, pray to be usable.

Pray to be Usable

Before Nehemiah was used to impact his generation in a positive, God-honoring way, we read that he mourned and fasted and prayed before the God of heaven (Nehemiah 1:4). Same was true for Moses: before he led the children of Israel into the Promised Land, he faithfully obeyed God's commands. As a boy, Billy Graham spent many an afternoon on the farm where he grew up reading the Scriptures and praying to God. Mother Teresa engaged in long periods of solitude and rest throughout her seasons of ministry.

Before God will move in our midst, you and I must be found usable too. What spiritual disciplines (such as prayer, Scripture-reading, fasting, solitude, service, etc.), do you practice to stay close to God despite the hectic pace of ministry? What impact does each discipline have on you? Note your responses on the chart on the following page.

HOW I STAY CLOSE TO GOD

Spiritual Discipline I Practice	Impact on My Life

Now consider how you, as a team, stay close to God. For example, some ministry teams share daily devotional readings or weekly chapel sessions. Note your team's practices in the space below.

Before moving on, write a brief prayer to God in the space below (or simply pray it) regarding your desire to be found usable for his purposes. Note any collective struggles your team is wrestling with that may prevent God from accomplishing his purposes in and through you.

Pray to Be Used

I have talked frequently about the buzz I feel when God uses me to help transform a human life—there is nothing else like it in any other experience this side of heaven. If you have been invited into his kingdom-building activity along the way, then you know exactly what I'm talking about. As you set about the tasks of finding and feeding holy discontent—in your own life, in the lives of your team members, and in your ministry as a whole—get yourself usable, and then beg God to actually *use* you. He really does desire your involvement in accomplishing his mission!

What would it look like if God was using you in the lives of those you lead and serve? If you were to articulate the way in which you want to be used in their lives in the space that follows, what would you say to God now?

How would you convey to God your desire for your *team* to be used in fulfilling his redemptive mission on earth? Jot down your prayer in the space below, or pray it to God verbally.

HOW MUCH SHOULD GOD'S MOVEMENT IMPACT YOUR VISION?

In addition to figuring out how to recognize God's movement, it is critical to know how much you should let the new movement impact your current vision.

My honest advice? As much as possible! Let me explain why.

In the mid-1980s, a few people who were passionate about global missions rallied together around that cause and formed an all-volunteer team. Eventually, the team developed into an ad hoc committee that established an overall missions strategy for Willow Creek, based on our core values. They facilitated work that was done all around the world, culminating in 2004 with Willow's formalized focus on the HIV/AIDS crisis in sub-Saharan Africa. In the last few years, our work in places like Zambia and South Africa has become so integrally involved with our overall strategy that we find ourselves upping the ante time and again to provide additional resources to the ministry and expose the cause to more and more people.

We have provided millions of dollars; thousands of care packs containing things like soap and toothpaste and clean socks; and scores of bicycles to villagers in the most remote regions of Africa. And it can all be traced back to a few people who refused to let their holy discontent die.

When the incorporation of our HIV/AIDS ministry was finally announced during our annual Vision Night one year, I remember thinking how anticlimactic it all felt. The movement was already underway! All I was doing was declaring the obvious: God was moving in our midst, and we were joining him.

Let me be perfectly clear: it is far easier and cleaner to maintain the status quo rather than to upset the apple cart by incorporating new ministries and ministry initiatives into your overall strategy. But to refuse to take the risk of enacting change that would ennoble holy discontent might just mean missing the very thing God is asking for you to accomplish.

• •

wrestle

When have you wrestled with whether or not to formally incorporate a new movement into your overall ministry strategy? What did you do?

What challenges or risks would you expect to face as you stay open to what God chooses to do through your team's passion pursuits? Note your response in the space below. For example, do you foresee having to give up control or the predictability of planning ahead? Might you face the risk of altering a brand-new vision just for the sake of going where God asked your team to go?

What about the opportunity side? What benefits or blessings might you realize as you stay open to holy-discontent-ennobling change in your particular ministry setting?

In *Holy Discontent*, I wrote that ministry leaders "steward the only message on planet Earth that can give people what their hearts need most, which is hope. Hope that sins can be forgiven. Hope that prayers can be answered. Hope that doors of opportunity that seem locked can be opened. Hope that broken relationships can be reconciled. Hope that diseased bodies can be healed. Hope that damaged trust can be restored. Hope that dead churches can be resurrected."[12]

This is the message we carry. This is the work we do. And Jesus never meant for this work to drain us, but rather, to fuel us. Lean into your holy discontent. Let it provide motivation for your cause, enthusiasm for your role, and energy for the tasks at hand. I am convinced that living and leading from holy discontent is the only way to experience what the apostle Paul calls "life that is truly life."[13] Personally, I wouldn't live life any other way.

ENDNOTES

1. Bill Hybels, *Holy Discontent* (Grand Rapids: Zondervan, 2007), 26.

2. Ibid., 26–27.

3. N. T. Wright, *Simply Christian: Why Christianity Makes Sense* (San Francisco: HarperSanFrancisco, 2006), 3. Emphasis added.

4. Hybels, *Holy Discontent*, 67.

5. Dan Allender, *Leading with a Limp: Turning Your Struggles into Strengths* (Colorado Springs: WaterBrook, 2006), 151. Emphasis added.

6. Robert Quinn, *Building the Bridge as You Walk on It* (San Francisco: Jossey-Bass, 2004), 36. Emphasis added.

7. Ibid., 19.

8. Hybels, *Holy Discontent*, 127.

9. Marlene D. LeFever, *Learning Styles: Reaching Everyone God Gave You to Teach* (Colorado Springs: Cook, 2001). Learning style descriptions adapted from chapters 3-6.

10. Matthew 10:8.

11. Hybels, *Holy Discontent*, 63.

12. Hybels, *Holy Discontent*, 148.

13. 1 Timothy 6:19.

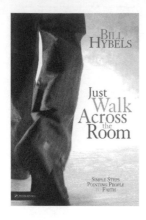

Just Walk Across the Room
Simple Steps Pointing People to Faith

Bill Hybels

What if you knew that by simply crossing the room and saying hello to someone, you could change that person's forever? Just a few steps could make an eternal difference. It has nothing to do with methods and everything to do with taking a genuine interest in another human being.

Bill Hybels shows how you can participate in the model first set by Jesus, who stepped down from heaven 2,000 years ago to bring hope and redemption to broken people living in a fallen world. The stakes are high. The implications are eternal. And you may be only a conversation away from having an eternal impact on someone's life—if you will just walk across the room.

Hardcover: 0-310-26669-6
Audio CD: 0-310-27223-8

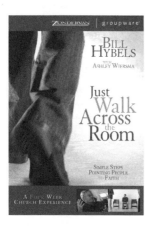

Just Walk Across the Room
A Four-Week Church Experience

Bill Hybels

Join thousands of churches nationwide in launching the complete four-week campaign experience based on the book *Just Walk Across the Room*.

The kit provides everything your church needs for four weeks of Sunday services and midweek small group discussions, including:

Kit: 0-310-27172-X
Participant's Guide: 0-310-27176-2
Small Group DVD: 0-310-27174-6

- CD-ROM
- Small Group DVD with Leader's Guide
- Participant's Guide
- *Just Walk Across the Room* Hardcover Book
- Quick-Start Guide

Pick up a copy today at your favorite bookstore!

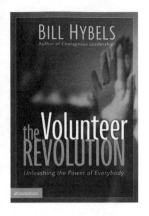

The Volunteer Revolution
Unleashing the Power of Everybody

Bill Hybels

"Imagine what would happen if people in our world took up serving towels and willingly—even joyfully—served other people in their everyday lives. Such attitudes and actions would change our world!"
—Bill Hybels

Drawing on years of leading volunteer teams, Bill Hybels explains how to give people freedom to discover their place of service in the local church, and how trained and committed volunteers can experience new joy and passion in serving Christ.

Hardcover: 0-310-25238-5
Audio CD: 0-310-25309-8

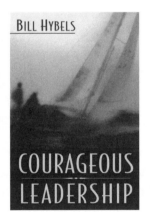

Courageous Leadership

Bill Hybels

Are you a 360-degree leader? Three-hundred-sixty-degree leaders don't just direct their gift of leadership south, to the people under their care. They also learn to lead north by influencing those with authority over them, and to lead east and west by impacting their peers. But most importantly, they learn how to keep the compass needle centered by leading themselves—by keeping their own lives in tune so they can provide maximum direction for others.

Bill Hybels shares lessons he has learned about the gift of spiritual leadership and its strategic importance within the church. Based on the thirty years he has led Willow Creek Community Church, this book is a must-read for all church leaders and their teams.

Hardcover: 0-310-24823-X

Pick up a copy today at your favorite bookstore!

Hardcover: 0-310-28306-X

When Leadership and Discipleship Collide

Bill Hybels

What do you do when the laws of leadership collide with the teachings of Christ?

Modern business practice and scholarship have honed the laws of leadership. To achieve success, you're supposed to—among other things—leverage your time, choose a strong team and avoid unnecessary controversy. But what happens when the laws of leadership and discipleship collide?

Using stories from his own life and ministry, Bill Hybels shows how the laws of leadership sometimes crash headlong into the demands of discipleship. And how the decisions you make at that point could affect not only you, but the destiny of those you lead.

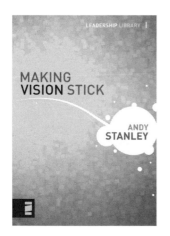

Hardcover: 0-310-28305-1

Making Vision Stick

Andy Stanley

Vision is the lifeblood of your organization.

It should be coursing through the minds and hearts of those you lead, focusing their creativity and galvanizing their efforts. Together, you and your team will strive to make your vision a reality.

But in order for that to happen, you've got to make your vision stick. That's your responsibility as the leader.

Pastor and author Andy Stanley first shows you the reasons why vision doesn't stick. Then, sharing vivid firsthand examples, he walks you through five simple but powerful ways to make your vision infiltrate the hearts, minds, and lives of those you lead.

Making Vision Stick provides the keys you need to propel your organization forward.

Pick up a copy today at your favorite bookstore!

LEADERSHIP DEVELOPMENT MATTERS

The Leadership Summit, a two-and-a-half-day event, convenes every August in the Chicago area and is satellite broadcast live to more than 135 locations across North America. Designed for leaders in any arena—ministry, business, nonprofit—its purpose is to encourage and equip Christian leaders with an injection of vision, skill development, and inspiration.

**For up-to-date information about The Leadership Summit,
visit www.willowcreek.com/summit**

This resource was created to serve you and to help you build a local church that prevails. It is just one of many ministry tools that are part of the Willow Creek Resources® line, published by the Willow Creek Association together with Zondervan.

The Willow Creek Association (WCA) was created in 1992 to serve a rapidly growing number of churches from across the denominational spectrum that are committed to helping unchurched people become fully devoted followers of Christ. Membership in the WCA now numbers over 12,000 Member Churches worldwide from more than ninety denominations.

The Willow Creek Association links like-minded Christian leaders with each other and with strategic vision, training, and resources in order to help them build prevailing churches designed to reach their redemptive potential. Here are some of the ways the WCA does that.

The Leadership Summit—A once-a-year, two-and-a-half-day learning experience to envision and equip Christians with leadership gifts and responsibilities. Presented live on Willow's campus as well as via satellite simulcast to over 135 locations across North America—plus more than eighty international cities feature the Summit by way of videocast in every fall—this event is designed to increase the leadership effectiveness of pastors, ministry staff, volunteer church leaders, and Christians in the marketplace.

Ministry-Specific Conferences—Throughout the year the WCA hosts a variety of conferences and training events—both at Willow Creek's main campus and offsite, across North America and around the world. These events are for church leaders and volunteers in areas such as group life, children's ministry, student ministry, preaching and teaching, the arts, and stewardship.

Willow Creek Resources®—Provides churches with trusted and field-tested ministry resources on important topics such as leadership, volunteer ministries, spiritual formation, stewardship, evangelism, group life, children's ministry, student ministry, the arts, and more.

Willow Creek Resources®—Includes substantial discounts to WCA training events, a 20 percent discount on all Willow Creek Resources®, *Defining Moments* monthly audio journal for leaders, quarterly *Willow* magazine, access to a Members-Only section on WCA's web site, monthly communications, and more. Member Churches also receive special discounts and premier services through the WCA's growing number of ministry partners—Select Service Providers—and save an average of $500 annually depending on the level of engagement.

For specific information about WCA conferences, resources, membership, and other ministry services, contact:

Willow Creek Association
P.O. Box 3188, Barrington, IL 60011-3188
Phone: 847-570-9812 • Fax: 847-765-5046
www.willowcreek.com

We want to hear from you. Please send your comments about this book to us in care of zreview@zondervan.com. Thank you.